The New Designer—Design as a profession
edited by the Bauhaus Dessau Foundation
(Regina Bittner, Katja Klaus, Philipp Sack) and
Catherine Nichols

Schools of Departure No. 2

T0044220

Article	Title/Author	Page

Table of Contents

Table of Contents

Table of Contents

PYTHAGORAS HYPOTENUSE SIMULTAN STIMMI
STIMULANZ KAUKASUS MEGAPHON EKLIPTIK ASTA

ASTROPHYSIK
OSCILLATION C
TRANSLATION
SAMARKAND
SAMARKAND

TASCHKEN
MOSKAU S
DESSAU OI
OPFER OP
MALARIA R
NEW-YORK
MEXIKO IK
KANADA DI

Travelling concepts beyond the Bauhaus

1

The Center of Industrial Design (Centro de Diseño, CDI), founded in Montevideo in 1987 in the context of so-called cooperation programmes, is regarded as a pioneering institute of modern design in Uruguay. In her thesis for the MA programme COOP Design Research at the Bauhaus Dessau, Lucia Trias, a former student of this new institution for modern designers, investigated how design knowledge was produced at the CDI. The establishment of this school for industrial designers, Lucia Trias deduced, was closely linked to development discourses that attributed a pivotal role to design in the modernisation of the South American nation. Here, the European modernist claim to universal validity as a model for economic and political progress in other regions was just as much part of the vocabulary of European 'experts' as the notion that design is inextricably linked to innovation, creativity and optimisation, and can contribute to the solution of economic problems. A view of design as a problem-solving activity, as it had been established in the West, was now also introduced as an instrument of aid delivery. New schools such as the CDI in Montevideo were assigned a key role in this.[1] Lucia's thesis, written in the historical Bauhaus Building nearly 100 years after the foundation of the avant-garde school, not only bears witness to the *longue durée* of the problematic narrative describing the designer's profession as an essential building block of industrial modernism, but also exposes the discipline's close interconnection with (neo-)colonialism and imperialism.

In the historical narrative, the Dessau Bauhaus is complicit in the evolution of those designers who, in the second half of the twentieth century, came to be criticised for their deeply problematic alliance with a consumer-centred society, as well as the reckless exploitation of natural resources and environmental destruction that came with it—an alliance that called for new blueprints for a socially responsible and environmentally friendly design. Victor Papanek (1923–1998) was among the early protagonists of a radical critique of consumerism and a rethink of the design profession as a social practice orientated towards the everyday needs of the masses. This included his engagement on behalf of regions then described as the 'Third World' and his advocacy

Specific conditions and types of knowledge are embedded in the DNA of this new design profession, projected in the discipline's convergence with Western industrial modernisations, consumer societies and technological progress.

for a shift towards local resources and local cultures of making. Contemporary social design and transition design movements build on the impulses that Papanek provided in the 1970s.

Common to all these criticisms is a desire to re-assess the problematic modern legacy of the design profession, which also involves the historical Bauhaus.

Walter Gropius had described the agenda of the Bauhaus workshops in Dessau as aspiring 'to produce designers that, through their knowledge of material and work process, were in a position to influence the industrial production of their day'. In fact, the Bauhaus was in step with a series of educational institutions questioning the new profession of the artist-designer in capitalist industrial production. The founding of schools of arts and crafts as imperial instruments to empower German industry on the global market and the collaboration with Deutscher Werkbund (German Association of Craftspeople) had already carved out a trajectory for the artist-proletariat—the 'surfeit' of students of over-filled art academies—and simultaneously paved the way for a new role for the artist, whose precarious position in the capitalist economy was now transformed into that of an avant-garde designer.

In this sense, specific conditions and types of knowledge are embedded in the DNA of this new design profession, projected in the discipline's convergence with Western industrial modernisations, consumer societies and technological progress. And it is precisely this model, perceived as universally valid, that was then exported worldwide by educators, in publications and other formats for academic exchange, which then caught on in newly established design institutions like the CDI. The reference to the authority of the Bauhaus played a pivotal role in this.

TRAVELLING CONCEPTS

The present book examines this intensely ambivalent evolution of the New Designer, deeply rooted in the logic of Western modernism, but without following the hegemonial narratives of linear design histories that frequently found their starting point in the avant-garde Bauhaus school. The volume, which originated in the context of the digital atlas 'Schools of Departure', rather considers itself to be an accumulation of contributions continuously producing new meanings and interconnections between schools, actors, objects, and ideas, thus enabling the development of a dynamic, virtual and open structure of interconnected learning as a transcultural practice. Indeed, this is the overarching objective of the entire series, which follows the branching paths of the development of the designer's profession in the context of new design schools.

In this series, the pedagogical approaches associated with the Bauhaus are not understood as a legacy in the sense of a tradition perpetuating itself, which revolves around the notion of an 'original' Bauhaus. Rather, the volumes published in the series draw on notions such as 'travelling concepts' and 'translation'. Learning experiments, ideas, materials, narratives and radical educational media move through time and space; however, this journey does not follow the linear notion claiming that these ideas are universally valid. Of interest here are the complicated and often bumpy paths of translation processes that, as Walter Benjamin proposed in his essay *The Task of the Translator*, only coincide with the original "just as a tangent touches a circle lightly and at but one point" and are likewise subject to transformation through time.[2] How can these 'acts of translation' in historical contexts be apprehended as continuous productions of meaning through contextual shifts? The volumes of this series are structured with reference to the discourses of travelling concepts of design and art education which, with always shifting connotations and attributions of meaning, keep the schools and initiatives in a process of constant exchange and motion. In the process, how do they resist the temptation of a concept of legacies that are linked with the Bauhaus tradition? By also bringing into view the divisions, the untranslatable, the faults that, as Doris Bachmann-Medick emphasises, place historical processes of change "in a tension-filled confrontation with contrasts and similitudes and, in doing so, bring into focus a fractured range of meanings through distortions of history".[3] In this sense, travelling concepts rather describe 'routes of appropriation' that do not follow the idea of a chronological sequence of past, present, and future, but move between different geographies, times and cultures. Thus, this book seeks to map the 'bumpy route' to the evolution of the New Designer with a network of knowledge regimes, technologies, economies, institutional frameworks, material cultures and social practices. In this respect, the individual contributions do not propose a straight-forward travel route that permits visitors to simply trace the movements that shape and discipline the designer through changing times, spaces and geographies. Instead, it is the diversions, dead-ends and misunderstandings, the distancing and the distortions that give voice to the multifarious movements in search of social and environmentally friendly design in both historic and contemporary transformation processes.

1   Lucia Trias. *Design Knowledges. Reflections on decolonizing design, looking at the role of institutions in the construction of design knowledge in Uruguay*. Master thesis. Dessau, 2019, p. 66.

2   Walter Benjamin. *The Task of the Translator*, http://www.ricorso.net/rx/library/criticism/guest/Benjamin_W/Benjamin_W1.htm, accessed 22 April 2023.

3   Doris Bachmann-Medick. 'Übersetzung zwischen den Zeiten. Ein travelling concept?', in: *Saeculum* 67/1, 2017, p. 42.

What might be truly social

2

"So, back in 1964, I resolved not to run on hatred",
writes Black feminist poet, activist, journalist and educator June Jordan, "but, instead to use what I loved,
words, for the sake of the people I loved. However,
beyond my people, I did not know the content of
my love: what was I *for*? Nevertheless, the agony of
that moment propelled me into a reaching far and
away to R. Buckminster Fuller, to whom I proposed a
collaborative architectural redesign of Harlem, as
my initial, deliberated movement away from the hate-
ful, the divisive."[1]

2

The "moment" Jordan is referring to, the one that
prompted her to reach "far and away" to Fuller, is
the very one that sparked the Harlem Riot of 1964:
when James Powell, an unarmed Black fifteen-
year-old boy, was fatally shot by a white police officer
on Manhattan's Upper East Side—only a few days
after Lyndon B. Johnson had signed the Civil Rights
Act. It was a period Jordan describes as the "zenith
of her preoccupation" with the visionary ideas of the
maverick architect, designer, philosopher, poet and
inventor.

Having long spent stolen free moments at The
Donnell Library, poring over books and losing herself in their pages "among rooms and doorways and
Japanese gardens and Bauhaus chairs and spoons",
Jordan had grown to believe in the transformative
possibilities of design. Immersing herself in the principles of Bauhaus practice, she had come to ponder
whether a spoon alone might indeed go some way
towards countering the "endlessly, dysfunctional

clutter/material of no morale, of clear, degenerating morass and mire, of slum, of resignation" affecting people living in poverty.[2] Yet her conviction that design could launch a social revolution was only truly cemented upon her 'meeting' Buckminster Fuller, also at the library: in the photographs she saw of his inventions, in the stories she read about his life and the writings of his she devoured, among them *Nine Chains to the Moon* (1938) and *Education Automation* (1962). Fuller's seldom-realised adventures in thought weighed upon her own "as a hunch yet to be gambled on the American landscape where, daily, deathly polarization of peoples according to skin gained in horror as white violence escalated against Black life".

A week after the riot, Jordan wrote a letter to a receptive Fuller, thereby launching a long-term collaboration in eco-social counter-design thinking that culminated in *Skyrise for Harlem:* a concrete plan to "obliterate the valley of shadows", to bring an end to the "self-perpetuating disintegration of walls, ceilings, doorways, lives" then home to a quarter of a million people, and to radically exorcise "a half century of despair" in a manner no "partial renovation" or "piecemeal healing" could ever achieve.[3] Rather than making urban renewal contingent upon the expulsion of residents, as was—and still is—common practice, their vision foresaw the construction of new dwellings above the moribund tenement buildings. Residents would remain living there until they could move up to their new home within a conical structure offering views from every window. The process, they anticipated, would take three years. And it would be participatory: Harlem residents would take part in the "birth of their new reality", a reality intended to reassure those who lived there "that control of the quality of survival is possible and that every life is valuable".[4] Upon completion of the elevated towers, the old buildings below would be demolished to make way for parks, open spaces, public seating and safer walkways. "No one", maintains Jordan in her article on the project for *Esquire* magazine, "will move anywhere but up."

At the time of its publication, Jordan's article met with widespread scepticism and some measure of derision; its content, though collaboratively developed, was ascribed to Fuller. Yet today the plan is coming to be regarded as a critical milestone in environmental design history, despite its never having come to fruition. For who other than Jordan, asks K. Wayne Yang, "has designed possibilities for Black life that keep Black communities intact, Black people emplaced, and Blackness integrated into the landscape? Check out her design, and decide if it looks like Wakanda to you too".[5]

What's at once intriguing and instructive about this "architextual collaboration",[6] about this poetic experiment in "comprehensive design", this revelatory exercise in design as dissent, as social responsibility, as revolution, are the multifarious insights it offers—and pivotal questions it raises—about the evolution of design as a profession. These insights, these questions might be thought of as a point of departure for the lines of enquiry gathered together within the present book, *The New Designer: Design as a Profession*.

The first such insight pertains to the role of the riot, indeed of crises—social, economic, political and ecological—in bringing forth and perpetually re-moulding the figure of the New Designer, a "social type, bearing a humanistic, universal outlook" and working towards "the benefit of humanity as a whole".[7] There is little consensus on what might be truly "social", on what could be truly beneficial to humanity, or on whether it even makes sense to think in terms of humanity "as a whole". Yet from Anni Albers to Arturo Escobar, few design theorists have felt inclined to dispute the impact of war, civil unrest and climate catastrophe on design pedagogy and practice.

Second, one might recognise that there is as much design to be found and learned from in slums and housing projects, in war and structural racism, as there is in Jordan and Fuller's *Skyrise for Harlem* or for that matter any other of Fuller's visions for Spaceship Earth. As Fuller's colleague and friend Victor Papanek demonstrated in *Design for the Real World*, design is inextricably bound up with social processes. It can both undermine and augment social justice. Yet more often than not it becomes a tool of technocracy or a catalyst of consumption, as opposed to an agent for social change.[8] For all their poetry and pertinence, benign observations, such as that of Cuban-born Mexican designer Clara Porset, about there being design in everything, "in a cloud… in a wall… in a chair… in the sea… in the sand… in a pot",[9] are of little consequence to thought if we fail to include in the list the iCloud… the Berlin Wall… the electric chair… the plastic ocean… sand erosion… potheads…

Third, one could discern the perceptible tension between competing visions of total design to have formed the New Designer, both of them differently lacking in self-reflection on their entanglement with capital and industry. Embodied in Jordan's intellectual transition from teaspoons to towers, from Bauhaus to Bucky as it were, it is a tension that, on one hand, reflects the successful export of Bauhaus thinking to all corners of the world. As Mark Wigley points out, and various contributions to the present journal discuss, not only were "objects designed, mass-produced, and disseminated; the designer himself or herself [was] designed as a product, to be manufactured and distributed. […] Even the teaching within the studios was a product. Gropius said that he only felt free to resign in 1928 because the success of the Bauhaus was finally established through the appointments of its graduates to teaching posts in foreign countries and through the adoption of its curriculum internationally".[10] Yet on the other hand, the faith Jordan placed in Fuller, with his rambunctious, all-encompassing philosophy of shelter and survival, speaks of a growing preference, shared by many, for his humane, humorous, hopeful brand of experimental interdisciplinarity. For all its overt fallibility, his

One should note the complex dynamics at work in design pedagogies—and in the ways in which these go down in history.

action plan to "make the world work for 100% of humanity, in the shortest possible time, through spontaneous cooperation without ecological offense or disadvantage of anyone"[11] took people's breath away.

Fourth, one should note the complex dynamics at work in design pedagogies—and in the ways in which these go down in history. Jordan learned about design from studying its products and the ideas that informed them in books held at the library. In a certain sense, she was not that different from Anni Albers and her fellow students at the Bauhaus in Dessau, who contrary to much myth and lore, claimed to have had no "education" as such. They had learned their craft not from listening to the "great masters", Wassily Kandinsky and Paul Klee, neither of whom ever deigned to speak to students, but from studying their works[12] and predominantly from "groping and fumbling, […] experimenting and taking chances" in a chaotic but stimulating laboratory-like situation.[13] Josef and Anni Albers, and indeed Buckminster Fuller himself, maintained that it was only in the United States, specifically at Black Mountain College that they gradually began to develop formal teaching methods—in constant exchange with their students and fellow professors. The same can be said of many of their Bauhaus-educated colleagues, whether they were teaching at Black Mountain or any of the other reform-oriented educational institutions scattered across the globe.

Though Jordan had never attended any design school, though she had had no formal exposure to modern or contemporary design pedagogies, she was able to bring to bear her self-taught knowledge of modern design in collaboratively redesigning Harlem from the ground up. With her extra-institutional trajectory, she was able to form a team with an esteemed, practising designer, who, as can be gleaned from their extensive correspondence, learned as much from Jordan's knowledge of sociology and political imagination as she did from his "Comprehensive Anticipatory Design Science".[14]

Until recently, all articles and exhibitions documenting the project attributed it solely to Fuller. Had Jordan, herself, not written of their collaboration in *Civil Wars*, we may still be waiting for the vital critical reappraisal that would return her silenced voice, her erased agency to a narrative so impoverished without her. This same reappraisal, which has gathered considerable momentum in recent years, confidently establishes Jordan as a "new designer" insofar as "she plots buildings and plots freedom".[15] It is a move that invites us to not only investigate the countless other protagonists and stories missing from the histories of design pedagogy, but also to rigorously rethink, as each of the contributors to this journal have been invited to do, how precisely the figure of the New Designer, this new "social type", has come into being—and to reimagine what she, he or they might embody today.

1   June Jordan. *Civil Wars*. Boston: Beacon Press, 1981, p. xi.

2   Ibid., p. xvii.

3   June Meyer (Jordan). 'Instant Slum Clearance', in: *Esquire*, vol. 63, no. 4, 1 April 1965, pp. 108–111. The original title of the article submitted by the author was 'Skyrise for Harlem', but the magazine changed it without consulting her to a title antithetical to the article's intention.

4   June Jordan. 'Letter to R. Buckminster Fuller' (1964), in: Jordan 1981 (as note 1), pp. 23–28, here p. 26.

5   K. Wayne Yang. 'Sustainability as Plantation Logic, Or, Who Plots an Architecture of Freedom?', in: *e-flux architecture* (October 2020), https://www.e-flux.com/architecture/the-settler-colonial-present/353587/sustainability-as-plantation-logic-or-who-plots-an-architecture-of-freedom/, accessed 26 September 2022. Wakanda is the fictional African nation ruled by Black Panther, the first African Marvel action superhero. The character and kingdom first appeared in the comic book *Fantastic Four*, no. 52 (July 1966)

and in 2018 in the superhero film directed by Ryan Coogler, the sequel to which—*Black Panther: Wakanda Forever*—has been released in November 2022.

6   Cheryl J. Fish. 'Place, Emotion, and Environmental Justice in Harlem: June Jordan and Buckminster Fuller's 1965 "Architextual" Collaboration', in: *Discourse*, vol. 29, no. 2/3, Special Issue: *Race, Environment, and Representation* (Spring and Fall 2007), pp. 330–345, here p. 331.

7   Reinhold Martin, writing specifically of the pedagogical approach taken by emigré professors László Moholy-Nagy and György Kepes at the New Bauhaus in Chicago, see Martin. *The Organizational Complex: Architecture, Media, and Corporate Space*. Cambridge, Massachusetts: MIT Press, 2005, p. 53.

8   See Alison J. Clarke. *Victor Papanek: Designer for the Real World*. Cambridge, Massachusetts, and London, UK: MIT Press, 2021, pp. 2–3.

9   Cited after Zoë Ryan (ed.). *In a Cloud, in a Wall, in a Chair: Six Modernists in Mexico at Midcentury*. Chicago: Art Institute of Chicago, 2019.

10   Mark Wigley. 'Whatever Happened to Total Design', in: *Harvard Design Magazine*, no. 5 (summer 1998), pp. 1–8, here p. 2.

11   Jaime Snyder quoting Fuller's 'mission statement for humanity' in his introduction to R. Buckminster Fuller, *Education Automation: Comprehensive Learning for Emergent Humanity,* Zurich: Lars Müller Publishers, 2010, pp. 7–26, here p. 24.

12   See 'Oral History Interview with Anni Albers', conducted by Sevim Fesci, 5 July 1968, for the Archives of American Art, in New Haven, Connecticut, online at https://www.aaa.si.edu/collections/interviews/oral-history-interview-anni-albers-12134, accessed 26 September 2022.

13   See Anni Albers. 'A Start', in: *On Designing*, Middletown, Connecticut: Wesleyan University Press, 1962, p. 36.

14   See Fish 2007 (as note 6), p. 342.

2

15 Charles Davis. 'Race, Rhetoric and Revision: June Jordan as Utopian Architect', in: Alice Y. Kimm and Jaepil Choi (eds.), *Open Cities: The New Post-Industrial World Order*, International Proceedings of the Association of Collegiate Schools of Architecture (ACSA) and Architectural Institute of Korea (AIK), Seoul 2014.

2

The School of Arts and Crafts in Bratislava (ŠUR): Educating anonymous, modern designers for practice

3

On 1 November 1928, when Bratislava's Chamber
of Trade and Industry offered three evening drawing classes in temporary premises, progressive profes-
sionals in the arts from all over Czechoslovakia
sat up and took notice—even though this news would
have normally only made the local daily paper. The
Prague journal of the Czechoslovakian work federation, *Výtvarné snahy* (Art Endeavours), supplied
an explanation for the optimism with which so many
suddenly looked to Bratislava: "These regular
evening courses were set up as a trial for a future
school of applied art",[1] reported the newspaper
all but immediately. If one considers, moreover, that
this story was about the very first public school
of art on Slovakian territory, it becomes evident why
such high hopes were riding on this initiative.

3

The launch of the drawing classes was preceded
by attempts over several years to reform arts and
crafts, or folk art, in Slovakia. These were sustained
above all by the Czech educational reformer and
future director of the school, Josef Vydra, who in a
first step was appointed head of the evening classes.
To a large extent, it is to his credit that even before
the planned *Škola Umeleckých Remesiel* (ŠUR,
School of Arts and Crafts) was founded, its resolutely
modern orientation had already been settled and
was maintained until its closure in 1939. The decision
about the foundation and curriculum of the school
had already been made in 1927 when the central

Czechoslovakian Ministry of Education invited all parties concerned to a meeting. Vydra was of course among them. Although it was agreed that Slovakia needed an art school, even at this stage the discussion was shaped by major discrepancies between progressive and conservative notions. Josef Vydra recalled the discussion as follows: "It was none other than the section head [of the Ministry of Education] Dr Zd. Wirth who spoke out against the creation of a new art academy and against the education of another 'artistic proletariat'. In his statement, he justifiably redirected the foundation and curriculum of the new school in Slovakia away from the envisaged academy of art to move along entirely different, practical lines."[2] The character of the first art school in Slovakia thus established from the start a bias against the so-called artistic proletariat, that is, the graduates of art academies, whose training was unsuitable for practice.

ALLIANCE WITH APPRENTICE SCHOOLS— A PROMISING EXPERIMENT

Despite ambitious plans and first formal steps, the process of founding the school threatened to collapse. As long as an appropriate building remained unavailable, it was hardly likely that the evening classes would evolve into a fullyfledged school of arts and crafts. The decisive impetus came in 1930 when the apprentice schools of Bratislava were relocated to a large, functionalist new building. Bringing the planned School of Arts and Crafts under the same roof as these appeared to be the ideal and only possible way to get hold of not only classrooms, but also well-equipped workshops. What is more, Josef Vydra, until then head of the Chamber of Trade and Industry's drawing classes, was appointed director of both schools.

Even though integrating the ŠUR in the apprentice school building was in the first instance a more or less pragmatic step, for Vydra this alliance formed the point of departure for a promising experiment. While throughout Europe, the merger of art academies and schools of arts and crafts would lead to a new type of art school,[3] for Vydra the answer, in Slovakia at least, lay in establishing the closest possible link between the apprentice schools and a progressive school of arts and crafts. The first profited from a general improvement of artistic standards among their graduates because the School of Arts and Crafts was to serve as a "rigorous reformer of taste" for the apprentice schools.[4] The chief advantage for ŠUR was the possibility of recruiting from the apprentice schools students with previous experience in workshops.

It is worth noting that at this time, there were some 2,500 apprentices in Bratislava.[5] With, among other things, the aid of a psychotechnical institute integrated in the school building, Vydra sought out from this mass the most talented individuals, who were offered an advanced course of art studies. This concept was enabled in part because, until its closure, the School of Arts and Crafts functioned

> The school is not and does not aim to be a
> copy of the once so famous Bauhaus,
> even if it followed its development keenly
> from the beginning.

3

mainly as an evening school, and the students thus
did not have to give up their main studies. Besides
the apprentices, for whom the courses were intended,
practically anyone with an interest in industrial arts,
craft or advertising could attend. Depending on their
skills, the students were divided into ordinary students with an apprenticeship diploma, exceptional
students without an apprenticeship diploma and
course participants.

Years later, Vydra continued to highlight the close link
with the next generation of skilled craftspeople, as
opposed to most art schools, which "merely worked
with the next generation of students".[6] He said:
"Outside Bratislava, just three contemporary schools

in Europe based their applied arts education on a previous knowledge of craftsmanship and an organisational link with vocational schools: the Bauhaus in Dessau, the School of Arts and Crafts in Brussels and the School of Arts and Crafts in Zurich, the latter two likewise in cooperation with apprentice schools."[7] In 1935, when confronted with the claim that he had established the Slovakian Bauhaus in Bratislava, he confidently stated: "The school is not and does not aim to be a copy of the once so famous Bauhaus, even if it followed its development keenly from the beginning. On the contrary, today it appears to be the more viable model due to its link with the apprentice schools, through which it found a closer connection to industry and production than the Bauhaus."[8]

EDUCATING ANONYMOUS, MODERN DESIGNERS FOR PRACTICE

The character of the School of Arts and Crafts in Bratislava was hugely influenced by the fact that Josef Vydra, as long as he maintained the practical and modern direction of the new educational institution, was more or less free to develop the curriculum as he saw fit and to select the staff he wanted. The lack of an art school tradition in Slovakia gave him the freedom to develop certain departments in the school without having to adhere to pre-existing structures. Under his leadership, the School of Arts and Crafts followed two basic lines. Firstly, by establishing departments that met the requirements of the curriculum of the apprentice schools,[9] and secondly, by responding to the growing intensity of city life and the current needs of the retail trade, which were frequently neglected by traditional schools of arts and crafts. As such, just one year after moving into the new building, the school established not only a variety of crafts departments (ceramics, wood, fashion and textiles) but also departments leaning towards the field of advertising (painting, graphic design, photography), as well as special courses for children.

3

In the 1934/35 academic year, a metal department and a window-display department were added. The latter in particular was an entirely new phenomenon which no other public school of arts and crafts in Czechoslovakia offered as an official subject.[10] But the final proof that Vydra's concept for the ŠUR was in tune with the latest trends came in the 1938/39 academic year, when a film department was set up for regular day-time students. At the time, this was the first and only public film school in Central Europe. Had the ŠUR not closed shortly thereafter, this would have enabled it to compete with even internationally recognised educational institutions and attract students from all over Europe.

In this manner, until its closure in June 1939, the School of Arts and Crafts in Bratislava resolutely pursued the policy of not educating another so-called artistic proletariat. Josef Vydra's art school model was not first and foremost about educating individual designers with artistic concepts of their own. Under the guidance of the school's progressive faculty,

Until its closure in June 1939, the School of Arts and Crafts in Bratislava resolutely pursued the policy of not educating another so-called artistic proletariat.

3

the students were required to understand the principles of modern design (for which they had to attend the obligatory class called 'contemporary taste'), to convert these into actual designs through practical work in the workshops and to ultimately put these into practice. At the same time, an emphasis was placed on experiments and on trying out new design approaches.

Modern techniques were also used to mitigate what was perceived to be a weakness of the student body: a lack of mastery in traditional drawing techniques. The school, as we must always remember, was working with the next generation of craftspeople, not artists. With this in mind, the so-called mechanised drawing method was introduced.

This method was developed at the school and utilised modern techniques like collage and frottage along with work with various templates to enable even less talented students or those without artistic training to follow a design process from beginning to end without the arduous work of drawing. Introducing the method at the 1937 International Congress for Art Education, Drawing and Applied Art in Paris Vydra postulated: "This modern epoch demands modern methods of teaching, rapid and economical. Mechanisation is at the school the process which permits contemporary progress to be followed. Mechanised drawing reduces both mental and manual action." [11] A few years later, he added: "These were simplified means of creative expression, suited to the shorter evening lessons." [12]

Even such thoroughly avant-garde approaches were implemented at the School of Arts and Crafts in Bratislava to educate designers with a modern approach who, in anonymous work, were to contribute through practice to the modernisation of Slovakia. To borrow the words of the Czech art historian and expert in the reform of art education in Czechoslovakia, Lada Hubatová-Vacková: "In the context of the reform ideals, the new generation of apprentices and students at the ŠUR should form a rank and file of nameless craftsmen capable of changing society by means of design." [13]

3

1   'Večerní škola kreslení Obchodní a živnostenské komory v Bratislavě', in: *Výtvarné snahy X*, 1928–1929, no. 8, supplement *Výtvarná výchova*, p. 84.

2 See *Strach z uměleckého proletariátu?* (Fear of the artist proletariat?), typescript, Moravské zemské museum, Brno, partial estate of Josef Vydra, box no. 59, p. 4.

3 For more information on the various attempts to merge art academies and schools of arts and crafts, see for example Julia Witt. 'Die Kunstakademiereform in der Weimarer Republik/Reforms of the Art Academies in the Weimar Republic', in: Simona Bérešová, Klára Prešnajderová and Sonia de Puineuf (eds.). *Škola ako laboratórium moderného života. K reforme umeleckého skolstva v strednej Európe (1900–1945)/School as a Laboratory of Modern Life. On the Reform of Art Education in Central Europe (1900–1945)*. Bratislava: Slovenské Centrum Dizajnu, 2020, pp. 78–94.

4 See 'Škola umeleckých řemesel v Bratislavě', in: *Výročná zpráva učňovských škôl a školy umeleckýchremesel v Bratislave* 1934/1935, p. 9.

5 See Jozef Vydra. 'Škola umeleckých remesiel a učňovská škola v Bratislave', in: A. S. Žitavsky (ed.). *Pamatnik slovenskeho školstva za učinkovania prezidenta T. G. Masaryka*. Bratislava, 1934, p. 116.

6 Ibid.

7 Josef Vydra. 'Počiatky prvej umeleckej školy na Slovensku. 30 rokov od založenia Školy umeleckých remesiel v Bratislave', in: *Výtvarný život* III, 1958, no. 8, p. 300.

8 'Škola umeleckých řemesel v Bratislavě' (as note 4), p. 9.

9 See František Reichenthal. 'Poznámky o vývine ŠUR v rokoch 1928–1938', in: *ARS* III, 1969, no. 2, p. 69.

10 See 'Škola umeleckých řemesel v Bratislavě' (as note 4), p. 8.

11 'The necessary link between Art and Technique. General report by H.-M. Magne', in: VIIth International *Congress for Drawing and Art Applied to Industry*, preliminary reports,p. 27.

12   Vydra (as note 7), p. 300.
13   Lada Hubatová-Vacková. 'Vzájmu dítěte, národa i státu. Vydrovy reformní aktivity v oblasti kreslení a uměleckého průmyslu', in: Klára Prešnajderová, Simona Bérešová and Sonia de Puineuf (eds.). *ŠUR. Škola umeleckých remesiel v Bratislave 1928–1939*. Bratislava: Slovenské centrum dizajnu, 2021, p. 271.

3

A New Deal for the New Designer: New York's Design Laboratory, 1935–1940

4

In the United States, the Bauhaus ideal of the New Designer first took root in the midst of the Great Depression, as the administration of President Franklin Delano Roosevelt responded to the protracted economic crisis with its New Deal program that included public employment initiatives, major infrastructure investments, and a basic system of social insurance. As part of the New Deal, in 1935 the Works Progress Administration's Federal Art Project (FAP) launched the Design Laboratory in New York City as the first comprehensive school of modernist design in the United States that was open to general enrolment. Like the Bauhaus teachers before them, the Design Laboratory faculty saw their mission as not just the development of a pedagogy and curriculum to train designers with technical proficiency in modern aesthetic trends, materials, and manufacturing methods, but rather to train designers who identified as agents of social transformation and reconstruction. Within the American context of the 1930s, their quest to create the New Designer was enmeshed within the broader struggles over the aspirations and limitations of New Deal social democracy. For its five years of operation, the Design Laboratory furnished a vibrant nexus between a novel public arts bureaucracy, the experimental modernism of the Depression-era avant-garde, the business culture of America's industrial design entrepreneurs, the militant labor unionism of the Congress of Industrial Organizations (CIO), and the political radicalism of the Popular Front social movement.

From the outset, the Design Laboratory's faculty, which included Bauhaus alumnae Hilde Reiss and Lila Ulrich, improvised in both their approach to design education and in their ongoing struggles to establish the school as a viable institution. In their focus on experimentation, they drew inspiration from the pragmatist pedagogy of John Dewey, whose educational innovations had also influenced the development of Bauhaus methods. Early coursework emphasized familiarity with a wide range of media and techniques, integrating multiple design skills in order to meet the needs of industry. In place of the "existing artificial distinction between interior decoration and the designing of mechanical objects", according to one of the school's initial bulletins, classes were "grouped according to present day trends in fabrication and design. In this manner, wood, metal and plastics are treated as a unit." As its first year drew to a close, it could still claim in a subsequent bulletin that the school was still the only one in the United States to "present in a coordinated fashion the standards of taste and style evolved elsewhere in the world in the so-called 'International Style'", even though its intention was not "to hand down dogmas about functionalism and modern design".

While the Design Laboratory owed its existence to the FAP, faculty and students soon found that their vision for the school's development was at odds with that of the agency's administrators. FAP director Holger Cahill and others in the agency hoped that the Laboratory would provide a source of competent personnel for its geographically dispersed programs to democratize American culture, but the school's faculty and students proved reluctant to leave New York for remote locales in the hinterlands. The status of the FAP as a temporary agency to alleviate the unemployment crisis also led to tension, as it compromised efforts to develop a multi-year curriculum for the Laboratory that would culminate in an academic degree, and it limited the school to hiring mostly individuals who met eligibility requirements for "relief" employment. By late 1936, faculty and students were organizing to establish the FAP on a permanent basis, and participating in militant demonstrations—including strikes and occupations—to try to win pay increases for public workers and prevent job losses. When the federal government curtailed funding for all

4

"The most beautiful architecture, design, and art is not built by the individual, but by the coordination of the talents and technics of individuals within the containing envelope of social relations."

New Deal programs, including the FAP, in mid-1937, the agency's administrators designated the school as one of the programmes to be eliminated.

Determined to see the Design Laboratory continue, a group of teachers and students, led by faculty chairman William Friedman, arranged for the Federation of Architects, Engineers, Chemists, and Technicians (FAECT), a radical, white-collar labor union affiliated with the newly formed CIO, to sponsor the school. Operation under union auspices was liberating in some key respects. In the fall of 1937, the faculty implemented a complete four-year curriculum that featured an introductory materials laboratory modeled on the Bauhaus preliminary course along with a two-semester design synthesis sequence intended to familiarise students with a diverse range of modernist styles and techniques. Faculty and students were also more closely aligned ideologically with the FAECT than with the FAP, and they refined their conception of the New Designer in the context of the radical politics of the Popular Front. The school's new declaration of principles asserted that "mass production, being dependent on mass consumption, necessitates designs to meet the social needs of the consumer". Designers were to place "as little emphasis as possible on ornament", avoiding "arbitrary" decorative elements that had "no genetic connection to the functional and mechanical properties of an object whose surfaces they adorn superficially". Art historian and critic Elizabeth McCausland, an ardent supporter of the Design Laboratory who eventually joined its faculty, avowed that "the original Bauhaus, germinal as it was, suffered somewhat from the romantically individualistic self-expression of the men of genius who founded and conducted it". By contrast, she continued, the Laboratory's faculty and students understood that "the most beautiful architecture, design, and art is not built by the individual, but by the coordination of the talents and technics of individuals within the containing envelope of social relations".

Freedom from FAP requirements also gave the Design Laboratory much greater leeway in expanding the faculty. The core group of instructors from the early days, anchored by Friedman, Reiss, painter Irene Rice Pereira, and product designer Jacques Levy, grew in the late 1930s to include McCausland, graphic design prodigy Paul Rand, muralist Burgoyne Diller, industrial designer Peter Schladermundt, painter László Matulay, and furniture designer Torben Müller among others. Enrolment, which had been robust under the FAP when courses were free, actually increased once the school began charging modest tuition under FAECT sponsorship, peaking at 400 students in late 1937. Unfortunately, the union's financial instability forced a second reorganization in 1938, with the school becoming an independent cooperative institution. Formally renamed the Laboratory School of Industrial Design, it received authorisation from the New York State Board of Regents to confer bachelor's degrees. Although the faculty continued to enhance and improve the pedagogy and

4

curriculum, the failure of a major fundraising drive in the fall of 1939 ultimately doomed the school, which was forced to suspend operations the following spring and return its charter to the state. Its faculty and students (most notably product designer Don Wallance and interior designer Suzanne Sekey) dispersed throughout America's culture industries and institutions of higher education, taking their experiences at the Laboratory with them to their future creative work as artists, teachers and critics during the middle decades of the twentieth century.

As our climate emergency of the early 21st-century leads to calls for a Green New Deal, the example of the Design Laboratory—and its mission of developing a New Designer capable of responding to complex social crises with a sustainable material culture for social democracy—remains highly relevant today.

4

Tomás Maldonado and his visual methodology in the context of the basic course at the Hochschule für Gestaltung Ulm

5

In his lecture on the occasion of the 1958 Brussels World's Fair, Tomás Maldonado (1922–2018) expounded on what may still rank as the cornerstones of the industrial designer's profession. The product designer, he predicted, "will be a coordinator. It will be his job to coordinate the diverse requirements of production and use in close collaboration with an array of experts. In short, he will be responsible not only for maximum productivity, but also for the greatest satisfaction of the consumer in both material and cultural terms."[1]

When Maldonado announced this prospect, he already had several years of teaching experience at the Ulm School of Design (Hochschule für Gestaltung, HfG) behind him. He had arrived at the new school in 1954 at the invitation of its founding director Max Bill, and by 1955, he was head of the basic course.[2] This class was obligatory for students in the first academic year or for those who had just newly arrived at the school.[3] When the HfG began teaching in temporary premises in August 1953, it was former Bauhauslers such as Walter Peterhans (1897–1960) or Josef Albers (1888–1976) who were asked to implement Max Bill's plan of re-establishing the Bauhaus in Ulm. Helene Nonné-Schmidt (1891–1976) was also chosen to support this objective. Even the founder of the preliminary course at the Bauhaus Weimar, Johannes Itten (1888–1967), was a guest lecturer at the HfG in late April 1955.[4]

Otl Aicher (1922–1991), co-founder of the HfG together with his later wife Inge Scholl (1917–1998) and Max Bill (1908–1994), had rejected the name Bauhaus Ulm for the HfG early on, during the founding phase. They decided instead to call it School of Design, thus adopting the subheading of the Bauhaus Dessau.[5]

The question of which pedagogical direction the HfG should take was discussed in the correspondence between Bill, Aicher and Scholl, as well as in Bill's exchanges with the teachers he wished to win over for the school. In a letter to Bill, Walter Peterhans speaks vehemently against the experiment, takes a swipe at the "Bauhaus kindergarten (or Bauhaus retirement home?)" and its pedagogy, and is ultimately fundamentally opposed to Bill's objectives.[6]

Josef Albers summarises his experiences of the two courses held at Ulm in a report to the Office of the High Commissioner for Germany, to whom he finally recommends further support for the ambitious project.[7] In his view, the teaching is founded on "vision and articulation". He rejects "self-expression" at the outset of an arts education, using a comparison with language to explain his rationale: To express oneself in a foreign language without the essential vocabulary is impossible; the same is true in the artistic field.[8]

To return to the opening quotation from Maldonado's Brussels speech, it behoves us to ask which demands might be made of the designer as coordinator, which range of subjects are required to prepare them for this role.[9] In Ulm, the school administration answers this question by introducing

5

subjects such as semiotics or mathematical operational analysis, to name but two.

In the basic course, this new approach is tangible as early as 1955. Tomás Maldonado names his component of the basic course 'Visual methodology', presumably in reference to Peterhans's 'Visual training', which the latter introduced in Chicago in 1938/39 and taught in Ulm in 1953.[10]

The assignments devised by Maldonado were clearly set out under the heading 'grundlehre 1955/56' by the student Klaus Franck (1932).[11] Most of the tasks are described in a short text, some have added explanatory sketches. Franck numbered the sketches from 0 to 8. Briefly, they are: '0 spinsky triangles' [!], '1 peano area', '2 weierstrass system', '3 black as colour', '4 symmetry', '5 precision—imprecision', '6 four exercises after ames', '7 five tasks on "equilibration of areas through colour and structural treatment"', '8', another group of three exercises without a common heading.[12]

The first study year, i.e., the basic course year, was dedicated to non-applied design—despite the students' desire to actually design something. The first priority was to learn about the foundations of design without having to think about utilizing the acquired knowledge.[13] Up to 1961, this basic course was the same for all, its completion being the prerequisite to student admission to one of the school's departments. From 1961, the general basic course was discontinued and organised in each department, thus being adapted to suit the respective subject (product design, visual communication, industrialised construction).

Tomás Maldonado, according to Aicher a "painting drop-out turned theorist",[14] was already preoccupied with theoretical questions during his time in Argentina, as William S. Huff verifies.[15] Huff, enrolled at the HfG in the 1956/57 academic year and an enthusiastic student of Maldonado's concept, refers to the four-volume book *The World Of Mathematics*, which is found in the surviving school library at the HfG-Archiv Ulm to this day.[16] These volumes include the essay 'The Crisis in Intuition' by the mathematician Hans Hahn.[17] The text begins with a critique of Immanuel Kant and his bias towards intuition and consequently cites numerous examples to prove that the then prevailing problems of mathematics could not be resolved through intuition. The evidence Hahn puts forward includes Weierstrass's concepts of a curve "that at no single point has a specific gradient, a specific tangent" and Giuseppe Peano and the continuous curve in the two-dimensional surface.[18] Even the curve, "all points of which are branch points" after the Polish mathematician W. Sierpinski, whom Klaus Franck misspells "spinsky" in task 0, is mentioned by Hahn.[19] Franck lists the Peano curve under Task 1, the Weierstrass curve under task 2. While this requires in-depth analysis to prove, it does indicate a pedagogical thrust that Maldonado summarised in his 1958 lecture like this: "We now know that theory must be combined with practice, and practice with theory. Today, action without knowledge

"Visual methodology is the principal subject of the basic course, the purpose of which is to train the students to adopt a deliberate and controlled approach to design processes."

is as impossible as knowledge without action. Operational scientific thought has vanquished the naive dualism, the pseudo-problems that so perturbed the first pragmatists." [20]

While this may be regarded as a critique that indirectly refers to the correspondence between Bill and Peterhans, when and to what extent Maldonado and Bill discussed these questions at the time admittedly remains open to question.

The lecture at the congress in Brussels mentioned at the beginning is of such critical importance for the further development of the HfG because it is in this lecture that Maldonado explained at length why the Bauhaus could no longer be a role model for the school. He wrote: "This educational philosophy is now in crisis. It is not able to absorb the new relationships between theory and practice established by the latest scientific development."[21]

1958 is the year in which the HfG took stock of its activities for the first time since its founding in 1953. On a total of 84 panels set up in the canteen of the school building designed by Max Bill, an exhibition designed by students and faculty documents the organisation and structure of the institution, the individual departments, the subjects of their classes, and more.[22]

Eleven of these panels are dedicated to the basic course.[23] Panel 97 shows the objective and the proportion of teaching given over to each subject. The basic course takes place during the first academic year and must be completed before the students can be accepted in one of the (as of 1958) only four departments. The text lists four objectives. Firstly, the basic course was to introduce the students to the work of the departments, especially the methods that are applied in each of them. The second objective seeks to compensate for the students' diverse educational backgrounds, for example, in terms of subjects studied or differing education systems in different countries of origin. The third objective "familiarises the students with the major questions of our technological civilisation and in this way conveys the horizons for the real design tasks of today". The fourth objective addresses interdisciplinary collaboration, which endeavours to ensure that "each individual understands the challenges and perspectives of the other collaborators". The two final objectives articulate the concept that will later become part of design history as the 'Ulm model'.[24]

Visual methodology was regarded as a major subject, as the allocation of class hours shows. It was allocated 420 hours, the work in the workshops by comparison only 280. Means of representation, which included design drawing, typography, language and fine art drawing, were allocated only 70 class hours, as are methodology, sociology and a range of scientific subjects, namely mathematics, physics and chemistry. Nonetheless, 140 class hours were allocated to twentieth century (sic!) cultural history.

Visual methodology, which is referred to on panel 100 as a main component of the basic course, is broken down on panels 100 to 107. On panel 100, the subject is described in more detail: "Visual methodology is the principal subject of the basic course, the purpose of which is to train the students to adopt a deliberate and controlled approach to design processes. In doing so, the ideas of the following scientific disciplines are to be taken into account:

1 cognition theory
2 symmetry theory
3 topology

[...] The course begins with elementary exercises from the field of visual perception. The tasks are resolved by utilising the findings of modern cognition theory."

Following this text, the other panels are dedicated to the following subjects: symmetry theory (T 101), cognition theory (T 102), design [and] structure (T 103), cognition theory (T 104), topology (T 105 and 106) and, finally, colour theory (T 107).

There is no sign of the Bauhaus-inspired tasks from the classes of Josef Albers or Walter Peterhans. Only the colour theory taught by Helene Nonné-Schmidt comes to light, in the 'Section through a colour sphere' on panel 107.[25] The renunciation of the Bauhaus, even in the basic course, is now finally complete.[26] For the New Designer, the way forward lies open.

The tasks are enumerated from 0 to 8.
maldonado course—basic course 1955/65
klaus franck

0

SPINSKY (SIC) TRIANGLE

5

01 schema the uniform colour grades specified in the scale are entered in triangles A, B and C in 3 different configurations. it appears that the optical effect of the colour grades differs in each of the 3 triangles and does not correspond with the scale.

02 grey-black

03 rectification grey-black in rectification, the colours in the triangles are optically aligned with the grades of the scale and obtain even increments.

04 yellow-red rectification by d. gillard
05 blue-white
06 blue-yellow

PEANO AREA

11 4096 areas; juxtaposed 64 times the module
according to schema c

WEIERSTRASS SYSTEM

21 based on an equilateral ▲ with 8 cm side
length the construction was arranged so
that the zig-zag lines fill a 32 • 32 cm square.
colour gradient: background: white-yellow-
white line: pink-purple-light blue
22 colour gradient: a) white-red-white: background / line: green b) white-blue-white:
background / line: orange

5

3

BLACK AS COLOUR

31 for composition, peano area was allied to c.
the 32 • 32 square was divided into 4 vertical
strips, the second of which is the inverse of the
first in terms of colouration. The colours are
interchanged in the third and the fourth is the
inverse of the third. / Black should not seem
like a 'hole' but have the effect of a colour.

40 shows the schema for 41 and 42 with an equilateral ▲ s = 1 cm a similarity transformation
is executed in such a way that one side length
has a ratio of 2:3 against the next biggest. The
transformation ranges from 1:1½ to 8:12. the second picture shows the inscribed circles of the
triangles

41 transparency through crosshatching. The described system is rotated by 180° and over-
lapped. the direction of crosshatching is rotated
by 90°.

42 illusory transparency and colour mixing.

43 katametry, similarity transformation of axis
systems.[Schema drawing] around a central
point, dots arranged at distances 1 2 3 4 are
themselves starting points for the configura-
tion of katametric figures, which from these points
likewise have the distances 1 2 3 4 on the
new axes. the connection consists of the common circumcircle.

51 symmetry: katametric figures, created by
turning a ray over a parallelogram.

53 [Schema drawing]: diameter 4 5 6 7 cm A3
format, developed from a square and its dia-
logues. Katametry

Exercises after ames demonstration depth graduation through colour treatment of planes

Harmonisation of planes through colour and structural changes

81 composition of 5–10 circle segments in a system of 20 circles

82 arrangement of 3 accents in each of 2 planes 20/20 each with 36 elements

83 3 overlapping systems 3 accents from each system form together a group by way of mutual colour

1	Tomás Maldonado. 'Neue Entwicklungen in der Industrie und die Ausbildung des Produkt-gestalters', in: *ulm*, 2, 1958, pp. 25–40, here p. 34 (lecture at the Brussels World's Fair, 18 September 1958).
2	HfG-Ar Sti PA 656/1.
3	For more information on the basic course at the HfG, see Angel Luis Fernández Campos. *Atlas propedéutico: El Curso Básico de la Hochschule für Gestaltung Ulm*, Madrid, 2018, unpublished dissertation, HfG-Ar bib 3.601.
4	For an overview see: HfG-Archiv Ulm (ed.). *bauhäusler in ulm: Grundlehre an HfG 1953–1955*, Ulm: HfG-Archiv, 1993.
5	Otl Aicher. 'bauhaus und ulm', in: *die welt als entwurf*, Berlin: Ernst & Sohn, 1991, pp. 87–95, here p. 87.

6	Letter from Walter Peterhans to Max Bill, HfG-Ar Sti PA 727, 4 September 1954.
7	Josef Albers. *Report on a Course in Basic Drawing, Design and Color given at the Hochschule für Gestaltung in Ulm*, dated 20 January 1954, addressed to the Office of the High Commissioner for Germany, HfG-Ar Sti AZ 0580.008, 9 pages, here especially section II, 'Principles Underlying my Courses at the Hochschule', pp. 1–3.
8	Ibid., p. 2.
9	On the development of the job description of the industrial designer at the HfG Ulm, see Dagmar Rinker. 'Produktgestaltung ist keine Kunst—Tomás Maldonados Beitrag zur Entstehung eines neuen Berufsbilds', in: Ulmer Museum/HfG-Archiv (ed.). *ulmer modelle—modelle nach ulm*, Ostfildern-Ruit: Hatje Cantz, 2003, pp. 38–49.
10	On Peterhans in Chicago, see Kristin Jones. *Visual Training at Illinois Institute of Technology: Aesthetics in Architectural Education*, Chicago, 2016, unpublished dissertation, HfG-Ar bib 3.267.
11	HfG-Ar, G 14, academic year 1955/56, ink on Schöllhammer card, 440 x 620 mm.
12	The original texts of the tasks are to be found in the addendum.
13	This corresponds with the approach of Josef Albers.
14	Aicher 1991, (as note 5), p. 92.
15	William S. Huff on the basic course in Ulm: 'Grundlehre at the HfG—with a Focus on the 'Visuelle Grammatik'', in: Ulmer Museum/HfG-Archiv 2003 (ed.), (as note 9), pp. 172–197, here p. 190. And again under this title with some different illustrations, in: Werner Van Hoeydonck/Christian Kern/Eva Sommeregger (eds.). *Space Tessellations: Experimenting with Parquet Deformations*, Basel: Birkhäuser, 2022, pp. 65–89.
16	James R. Newman. *The World of Mathematics*, 4 volumes, New York: Simon & Schuster, 1956, HfG-Ar 51 Wor 1–4.

5

17	Hans Hahn. 'The crisis in Intuition', in: Newman 1956 (as note 16), vol. 3, pp. 1956–1976. First published in German as 'Die Krise der Anschauung', in: *Krise und Neuaufbau in den exakten Wissenschaften. Fünf Wiener Vorträge*, Leipzig / Wien, 1933, pp. 41–62.
18	Hahn 1933, (as note 17), pp. 51–52.
19	Ibid., pp. 58–59.
20	Maldonado 1958, (as note 1), pp. 39–40.
21	Ibid.
22	HfG-Ar Sti T 093-T 177. This and other exhibitions are the subjects of two informative dissertations that emerged from the HfG research project 'Gestaltung ausstellen. Die Sichtbarkeit der HfG Ulm: von Ulm nach Montréal', sponsored by the Volkswagen Foundation. Christopher Haaf. *Von Ulm in die Welt. Ausstellungen der HfG Ulm*, Leipzig: Spector, 2023; Linus Rapp. *Wohltuende Sachlichkeit: Ausstellungsgestaltung an der HfG Ulm*, Leipzig: Spector, 2023.
23	HfG-AR Sti T 97–107. Mixed image and text panels, text-only and image-only panels.
24	For further information, see Ulmer Museum/ Hfg-Archiv 2003 (as note 4).
25	HfG-Ar Sti T 107, photograph of the sheet produced by Helmut Müller-Kühn.
26	Maldonado 1958 (as note 1), pp. 39.

noigandres 4

poesia concreta

An essay by Ilana S. Tschiptschin

Words and worlds: The poetry of design between Brazil and Germany

6

The first contacts between Brazil and Germany in the domains of art and design took place mainly through São Paulo Biennials, the *Museu de Arte de São Paulo* (MASP, São Paulo Museum of Art) exhibitions and its *Instituto de Arte Contemporânea* (IAC, Institute of Contemporary Art), considered to be the first design school in Brazil. In 1953, coinciding with the inauguration of the HfG Ulm, Max Bill participated in the jury of the second São Paulo Biennial[1] and connected Brazilian artists with Ulm and its ideals. From 1953 to 1956, six Brazilian artists and designers, among them Almir Mavigner, Mary Vieira, Alexandre Wollner and Yedda Pitanguy,[2] studied at the HfG Ulm, becoming pivotal in several connections that would unfold between the two countries.

Meanwhile, during the 1950s, discussions involving Max Bill were held about the possibility of creating a design school at the *Museu de Arte Moderna do Rio de Janeiro* (MAM-RJ, Museum of Modern Art in Rio de Janeiro), for which Tomás Maldonado was assigned to write a curriculum proposal. Although the *Escola Técnica de Criação* (ETC, Technical School of Design) never came into being, courses and lectures did take place at MAM-RJ, including a visual communication course co-taught by Maldonado and Otl Aicher.

In the early 1960s, the *Escola Superior de Desenho Industrial* (ESDI, School for Industrial Design) was founded in Rio de Janeiro, and its first curriculum both referred to Maldonado's plan for the

ETC-MAM school and adopted the scientific approach that was prevailing in Ulm. Alexandre Wollner and Karl Heinz Bergmiller, former Ulm students, were among its founders. The German theoretician and HfG professor Max Bense taught several courses at ESDI, where the concrete poet Décio Pignatari also worked as a professor of information theory.

CONCRETE ART—
AN AUTONOMOUS OBJECT

In these exchanges one can follow a constant concern with the investigation of non-discursive languages for which concrete art marks a fundamental moment. At the same time it appears as a first point of intersection between Brazilian and German artists during the 1950s. Based on a self-referential vocabulary of a purely plastic materiality (lines, planes, and colors), concrete art ceased to be a representation of reality outside the canvas and became the presentation of its own structural instrumentation. For its exponents, the essential aspects of visual art were matter, space-time, and movement. Art was considered a form of knowledge, and the artwork an autonomous object. The movement defended a universalist aspiration, postulating that this practice, through the search for a collective meaning and the collaboration with industry and the mass media would reach the sphere of the everyday, unifying art. Thus, design played a fundamental and inseparable role in this concept of art.

As in the field of concrete art and design, concrete poetry was based on the resumption of a constructive corpus that revolved around the European avant-garde, mainly the De Stijl movement and the Bauhaus school,[3] establishing tight relationships with contemporary experimentation in other fields such as music, painting, architecture and design. This tradition finds its expression in poets' productions through the incorporation of a structural and materialist line of thought and the defense of the use of mass communication.

In 1952, Décio Pignatari and the brothers Augusto and Haroldo de Campos formed the group *Noigandres*,[4] decreeing an end to the historical cycle of the verse and exploring the concrete graphical space of the page as a poetic practice.

In 1953, during a visit to the Brazilian students at the HfG Ulm, Décio Pignatari met the Bolivian-Swiss poet Eugen Gomringer, Max Bill's assistant at the time. For Gomringer and the Brazilian poets, poetry was to be constituted by the simplest structure based on the relationships between words rather than their discursive juxtaposition, with the former being called 'constellation'[5] and the latter 'ideogram.'[6]

The word in its three dimensions—spatial-graphic, acoustical/oral and semantic—was considered as an autonomous 'thing-word' and poetry turned into a 'verbivocovisual'[7] system, defined as a specific linguistic area that used the advantages of the simultaneity of verbal and nonverbal communication.

Moreover, the thing-word was seen as a living organism or a living system—"the concrete poet sees the word itself […] as a dynamic object, a living cell, a complete organism, with psycho-physical-chemical properties, tactile antennae of circulation heart: alive."[8]

LANGUAGE AS DESIGN

The cooperation between Décio Pignatari and Eugen Gomringer unfolded in several ways. One of these was the encounter between the Brazilian concrete poets and HfG Ulm professor Max Bense who together with his colleague, the semiotician and publisher Elisabeth Walther[9] would organise several exhibitions and publications about Brazilian poetry, art, and design in Stuttgart, besides writing a philosophical travel report, *Brasilianische Intelligenz: Eine cartesianische Reflexion* (Brazilian intelligence. A Cartesian reflection), as a result of his close interactions and five visits to Brazil.[10]

Bense, whose work focused on the relationship between aesthetics and technology, developed a rational aesthetic defining the components of the text, be it utilitarian or literary, as a repertoire of statistical language built according to information measurements as opposed to semantics.

An approximation between Max Bense's design theory and those of the Brazilian concrete poets becomes clear in the procedures proposed by the former in the experimental curriculum for HfG Ulm's information department:

"Conversion of natural languages and artificial languages into precise languages. Experiments on grid systems, shortening techniques and montage techniques. Concentration and dispersion of form and topics. Syntactic and semantic shortening, compression, distortion, lengthening, alienation. Accidental and attributive descriptions, phenomenological reduction and deflation of meaning." [11]

For Bense the word should not be used as a carrier of intentional meaning but as an element of material design, so that meaning and design (Gestaltung) are mutually conditioned and expressed. [12] Likewise, for Brazilian concrete poets the word was a purely objective thing, free from redundancies and inaccuracies, with the poem perceived as an experimental search for clarity and integrity in language. Poets strove to create an economic structure, analogous to the speed of modern communication and technology, prefiguring the poem's reintegration into everyday life—similar to how the Bauhaus approached the visual arts—either as a vehicle for commercial advertising or an object of pure enjoyment. In either case, the aim was to approach the word, in an elementary sense, as if it were being heard for the first time.

In search of a non-discursive language, poetry revealed the capacity of language-as-design:

"Our century is the century of planning, of design and designers: industrial design and architecture are studied and projected as messages and as languages; writers, poets, journalists, advertisers, musicians, photographers, filmmakers, radio and television producers, painters and sculptors are beginning to become aware of designers, forgers of new languages."[13]

1   In 1951, Max Bill's first exhibition in Brazil opened at the MASP, with participation by IAC students, and in the same year Bill won the sculpture prize for his work titled *Tripartite Unity* at the first São Paulo Biennial.

2   The two others were Elke and Frauke Koch-Weser, who had grown up in Brazil as daugthers of German parents. Later, Isa Maria Moreira da Cunha, Mario Zocchio, Jorge Bodanzky, and Günter Weimer also studied there. See Martina Merklinger. 'Arena of Modernism: The Founding Years of the São Paulo Biennial and the Foreign Cultural Policy of the Young Federal Republic of Germany', in: Ulrike Groos/Sebastian Preuss/Institut für Auslandsbeziehungen (eds.). *German Art in São Paulo.* Ostfildern, Hatje Cantz, 2013, p. 41.

3   See Gonzalo Aguilar. *Poesia concreta Brasileira: as vanguardas na encruzilhada modernista.* São Paulo, 2005, p. 39.

4   The term 'Noigandres' was taken from Ezra Pound's *Canto XX,* as "a synonym of poetry in progress, as a motto of experimentation and poetic research collaboratively". Noigandres was also the name given to the group's publication. Augusto de Campos/Haroldo de Campos/Décio Pignatari. 'Sinopse do movimento de poesia Concreta', in: *Teoria da Poesia Concreta,* São Paulo, (2) 1975, pp. 193–206, here p. 193. 3. https://monoskop.org/images/1/1f/De_Campos_Pignatari_De_Campos_Teoria_da_poesia_concreta_Textos_criticos_e_manifetos_1950-1960_2a_ed.pdf, accessed 11 May 2023.

5	Eugen Gomringer. 'From Line to Constellation', in: Mary Ellen Solt (ed.). *Concrete Poetry: A world view*. Bloomington: University of Indiana Press, 1968, http://www.ubu.com/papers/gomringer01.html., accessed 11 May 2023.
6	The concept, extracted from Ezra Pound's 'ideo-grammic method', was based on his study of *The Characters of the Chinese Language* as a Medium for Poetry by the American orientalist and art critic Ernest Fenollosa. In this process of composition, two things combined do not produce a third, but rather suggest a fundamental relationship between both. By doing so, the Chinese ideogram brings language close to things. See Haroldo de Campos. 'Aspectos da Poesia Concreta', in: de Campos/Pignatari/de Campos 1975 (as note 4), p. 138.
7	The term 'verbivocovisual' is a neologism coined by James Joyce. As appropriated by the concrete poets, it indicates the interweaving of the visual, vocal, and verbal dimensions of language in poetic creation.
8	Augusto de Campos, 'Poesia Concreta', in: de Campos/Pignatari/de Campos 1975 (as note 4), p. 44.
9	The German theoretician Elisabeth Walther was a member of the Stuttgart group alongside Bense, and other writers and theorists. She taught at HfG Ulm, University of Stuttgart, and ESDI.
10	In 1961 Max Bense visited Brazil for the first time; in the following year he and Elisabeth Walther published the *Noigandres / Konkrete Texte* anthology; in 1963 Júlio Medaglia organized the exhibition *Konkrete Dichtung aus Brasilien* at the University of Freiburg, and Max Bense promoted a new exhibition of concrete Brazilian poetry in the Eggert bookstore in Stuttgart. Bense also organized several exhibitions of Brazilian artists in the Studiengalerie Stuttgart, such as *Concrete Poetry* (1959), and shows with works by Almir Mavigner (1957), Bruno Giorgi (1962, 1966),

Alfredo Volpi (1963), Lygia Clark (1964), Aloísio
Magalhães (1965), Mira Schendel (1967), and
Fonseca, Azevedo, Torres e Ianelli (1968), almost
all accompanied by an edition in the *rot* series.
Max Bense, Elisabeth Walther, and Haroldo de
Campos started corresponding in 1959 and con-
tinued to do so until Bense's death in 1990. For
an overview on the subject see: Nathaniel Wolfson.
'A Correspondência entre Haroldo de Campos,
Max Bense e Elisabeth Walther: Uma primeira lei-
tura', in: *Circuladô*, 2 (2), October 2014,
pp. 79–94.

6

11   Max Bense. 'Texte und Zeichen als Information', in:
        Texte und Zeichen: Eine literarische Zeitschrift,
        2 (4), 1956, pp. 437–440. Cited in: David Oswald.
        'The Information Department at the Ulm School of
        Design', paper for the 8th Conference of the
        International Committee for Design History &
        Design Studies, São Paulo, 2012, p. 4.

12   Max Bense. 'Konkrete Poesie', in: *rot* 21, Stuttgart,
        Mai 1965. On this issue, see also Elisabeth
        Walther. 'Max Bense's Informational and Semiotical
        Aesthetics.' http://www. stuttgarter-schule.de/
        bense.html, accessed 11 May 2023. The search for
        a relation between sensitivity and rationality is
        what motivated Bense's attention to Brazilian mo-
        dernity, explored further in his book *Brasilian-
        ische Intelligenz: Eine cartesianische Reflexion*,
        Stuttgart: Limes, 1965.

13   Décio Pignatari. *Informação, Linguagem,
        Comunicação*, São Paulo: Cultrix, 1981, p. 15.

Bill Howell

Alex Walker

1. Poster for Pamoja Gallery. Designer:
   Bill Howell.
2. Symbol sketch for Product Engineering
   magazine (not used). Designer: Alex Walker.
3. Symbol for Island Record Co. Designer:
   Alex Walker.

1.

designer often sidetracks into freelance work; a few black designers in New York have sidetracked permanently, opening up their own design studios. This was the case with William Wacasey, who worked his way through the usual channels of lettering and display man for retail outlets and packaging/product designer for an industrial design firm before opening Wacasey Associates—New York's first black-owned design studio—only to discover initially that "because I was black I tended to get the smaller jobs or those with practically no budget."

Alex Walker opened his own design studio last year, after leaving a position with a studio which he had held for 13 years. This long stay with one firm is not unusual; when a black designer gets a job in the design field he tends to keep it, knowing there is not an over-abundance of positions available to him. Looking back on his own experience, Walker states, "Unusually long periods of employment at one job tend to hamper one's creative processes. Most white designers who eventually become award-winning art directors or make lots of money spent short periods of time in various studios and agencies. With each move, their knowledge, contacts, and usually their incomes increased. This is one modus operandi that has left the black designer in the dust."

One reason black designers don't move around more is that they lack the all-important contacts in the field through whom job openings are referred. In his anxiety simply to get any work in the field, a black designer may get tied down to a department store or supermarket advertising department. Stuck in this backwater, he never gets to meet people in the mainstream and thus is unable to find out what is expected of a designer in a large-agency art department.

Dorothy Hayes raises an interesting—if painful—point.

"We're all in this big conversation" —Design as plurivocality

7

CATHERINE NICHOLS Dear Lesley-Ann, I was always planning to start this discussion by quoting the legendary designer and DJ Virgil Abloh, who imagined design pedagogy and practice as inherently plurivocal. He thought of everyone as being in one big conversation. Scrolling through articles on *The Guardian* app this morning, though, I serendipitously stumbled across an article by Zadie Smith on the rerelease of Gretchen Gerzina's milestone history *Black England: A Forgotten Georgian History,* for which Smith has written the foreword.

As Smith, a well-known novelist, essayist and professor of creative writing, points out, Gerzina's milestone book highlights and redresses the erasure of Black people and their achievements from British history. When she first read the study back in the 1990s, it profoundly influenced her self-understanding and development as a writer.

If I was half asleep when I started reading the article this morning, I was certainly wide awake by the end—because the content resonated so strongly with the tenets of many of your projects and the questions I wanted to discuss with you.

Indeed, the article drives home the point that you and your colleagues so pertinently make in *The Black Experience in Design: Identity, Expression and Reflection* (2022), namely that white cultural supremacy in education brings forth impoverished, skewed narratives that distort history and ultimately stifle creativity. It shuts down the "big conversation" that Abloh was speaking of, or at least prevents it from flourishing.

How did *The Black Experience in Design*, a project that seeks to both revise and re-envision the past, present and future of design education, come about?

7   LESLEY-ANN NOEL I am one of six editors of The Black Experience in Design. The other editors are Anne H. Berry, Kelly Walters, Jennifer Rittner, Kareem Collie and Penny Acayo Laker. The project was Anne H. Berry's brainchild. I think Kareem called me and asked me if I'd be interested in joining. When we all met, we brainstormed about how to respond as design educators to the interest in Blackness in design. Anne and a few of the others were interested in writing the book that they yearned for when they were design students. I was tired of questions like "where were all of the black designers?" and excited to create a space where we could challenge those types of questions and show that Black designers are here, can tell their own stories, and are doing exceptional work. Personally, I found the question very White-centric. There are Black people doing design work, but I felt that the people who were asking the question were being lazy, and not looking in the right places. We talked about several different formats. We seriously considered a special issue of an academic journal, but we quickly recognised there were too many people we wanted to invite to contribute, and a journal would only accommodate six to eight essays,

so the idea morphed into a book. One of the editors knew Steven Heller, who was generous enough to meet with us and talk through the idea. We created a few lists of people we'd want to be represented within a 'textbook' about Black design, and we considered several different formats. We had some guiding principles about representing a range of disciplines within design, a range of identities, the authentic voices of the contributors, and about creating many different means of being a contributor, from poetry to essays, from images to conversations and more.

CN Throughout your academic career you have worked extensively to broaden conversations around design practices and histories, to include multiple voices and perspectives coming from outside 'dominant' design culture. Here I'm thinking in particular of your experience as convenor of the Design Research Society's *Pluriversal Design Special Interest Group* (PluriSIG). To what extent did your prior research flow into—and perhaps prepare you for the outcomes of—The Black Experience in Design?

LAN My previous research and the work with the Pluriversal Design Special Interest Group had a huge impact on my process within this project. When I started, I was a professor of practice at Tulane University in New Orleans, and we had worked for two years on the podcast *Hello from the Pluriverse*, which featured student interviews with designers around the world. That podcast was tied to one of

PluriSIG's aims of shining a light on the wide diversity of design practices around the world. The Black Experience in Design was also published after the Pivot 2020 conference, a conference in which we had many conversations about shifting centres, methods, epistemologies and ontologies in design. What I/we learned from the podcast and the conference were strategies for supporting people as they told their own stories and ensuring that these stories were accessible in traditional academic formats. In both projects we created many different ways of participating, such as conducting and recording interviews and then downloading and publishing transcripts or transforming them into essays. So, by the time I joined The Black Experience in Design team, I knew that we could move beyond traditional academic publication barriers to make sure we had the participation of many voices in the work. I'd say that my previous work prepared me for the process, more than the outcomes. I used strategies that I learned from previous research in my role as editor and led writing groups for contributors, provided writing prompts, did interviews with those who didn't have the time to write, ghostwrote articles based on interviews, etc. I'd say that is, in part, why we were so successful in collecting so many stories. There were so many ways to contribute to this work.

My research and the corresponding research methods often focus on emancipation and liberation. I'm very satisfied with the outcome of the work, because this is a book about Black creatives by

Black creatives in which close to seventy Black designers tell their own stories. It's a 'for us, by us' emancipatory and liberating work. I'm very proud of having played a role in making this possible.

CN   Were there voices in the anthology that surprised you?

LAN There are so many stories in this work that it's hard to single out what might have surprised me. The voices in the anthology provoked a range of emotions for me. So, I suppose that "surprised" might be a word I'd use, but I also felt seen and validated by the familiarity of themes in some of the stories. The Ghanaian-South African professor Nii Commey Botchway made me reflect on what Blackness is and what design is. Steve Jones's essay speaks directly to the experience of many Black design students at a predominantly White institution, where a professor gives a sometimes unintentionally exclusionary assignment prompt. Kaleena Sales shares reflections on what it means to be a Black design educator teaching mainly Black students at a historically Black university. It is not a privilege that many Black design educators have in countries where they are part of a minority group. The way in which she has wrestled with the way she used to teach them to fit into a White world was very poignant. I really enjoyed Lauren Williams' manifesto for Black women in academia, maybe it hit too close to home! I was privileged to have a seventeen-minute conversation with

> The history of the discipline can seem exclusionary for many Black designers. The new methods that these designers and educators propose do not necessarily have to build on historical approaches. As outsiders or people who are othered, they can see keenly what is needed for them to thrive and then propose methods that fill those gaps.

adrienne maree brown that led to her contribution. She gives great advice for Black designers, to listen for design within themselves, to think about abolition, to read Audre Lorde! I love the ending of her piece: "Have a really massive vision! Because I do think that this is our time." If I had to recommend that people read one essay, I'd say read brown's because it is so hopeful, but it's hard to recommend only one.

CN In the book, Maurice Cherry—creator, producer and host of the groundbreaking podcast series on Black designers, *Revision Path*—contends that "merely celebrating yourself as a Black designer is an act of rebellion". Such "rebellion" is crucial if design education is to become truly social. Yet the scope of the book extends well beyond the celebration of Black designers and histories of resistance. Indeed, it simultaneously explores innovative methods and models for design teaching and research. And it reimagines learning institutions as non-hostile, liberatory spaces. What kind of historical approaches do such new methods build upon?

LAN This is a difficult question. There are some authors who lean more intentionally into history in their work, such as David Pilgrim, who uses historical objects to teach social justice. Colette Gaiter tells her story using images from the past, especially the 1960s and '70s. Alicia Ajayi writes about the design of 'free papers' which were artefacts that guaranteed the free passage of the formerly enslaved.

The history of the discipline can seem exclusionary for many Black designers. The new methods that these designers and educators propose do not necessarily have to build on historical approaches (if I'm understanding the question correctly). The ones with formal design training may be instinctively building on their training, but might also be reacting and rejecting it, because they have been able to see gaps in the historical approaches of design. As outsiders or people who are othered, these designers and educators can see keenly what is needed for them to thrive and then propose methods that fill those gaps.

Some of the new methods are proposed by people who do not have formal design training, but who operate within the world of design. They are drawing from their lived experiences, approaches from other disciplines, their social experiences of community, collaboration, inquiry and more. Chris Rudd shares a syllabus from his class. In his essays he talks of complicating Bauhausian traditions by weaving in indigenous practices. His reading list includes texts on race, class, feminism, and politics, and he is advocating for a more critical perspective in design.

CN Speculative narratives, whether historical or futuristic, also play an important role in evolving emancipatory educational spaces…

LAN I edited the section specifically about futurism, but I do believe that a conviction that we deserve better and that we can make better for ourselves (nobody else has to save us) drives the development of emancipatory new approaches and new spaces. Something that really bothered me in 2020 was the way the questions about "where are the Black designers and how can we help them" were asked. What I loved about the accounts in chapter 8 are the stories of defiance and agency. They are inspiring stories of how people started their own spaces, such as Maurice Cherry's Revision Path podcast, Moline's Facebook group and web platform for *African American Graphic Design* and Malene Barnett's *Black Artists and Designers Guild*. Some of the essays in the futurism section could just have easily been placed in the chapter on radical and liberatory spaces because the contributors like Lonny Brooks, Woodrow Winchester III, Adah Parris and John Jennings are in fact using futurism to evolve their work, and for themselves and others to imagine new spaces and practices.

CN One concrete product of your research has been the *Designer's Critical Alphabet*, a deck of cards and a digital app you created in 2019. You have described the cards as a tool to help train design students, educators, researchers and practitioners to sharpen their critical awareness of design histories, pedagogies and practices, to reflect on diversity and inclusion.

7

Could you please tell us a little bit about the project and the ways in which the contemporary world as a whole might benefit from unlearning exclusive epistemologies and methodologies? What do human and more-than-human beings stand to gain from pedagogies at once plurivocal and pluriversal?

LAN Oh my, you ask difficult questions. The aim of 'the Designer's Critical Alphabet, and the follow-up *Good Vibes Deck,* is to encourage people to ask more questions. I say all the time, "Question everything! Nothing is sacred!" So, these tools have introductory critical questions. The idea is not that these are the only critical questions that people must ask, but that the deck can encourage people to remember to ask and reflect on questions about race, gender, language, politics, and even to reflect on their own positionalities and self-awareness in the work that they do as designers. Hopefully, where there may be pressure to flatten and simplify, the alphabets will encourage people to complicate, sit with the discomfort that complexity can bring and use this to gain a deeper understanding of the problem area that they may be focusing on. What do we all stand to gain from pluriversal pedagogies? On a 'feel-good' level we all gain from being able to learn from the richness of the many different perspectives that people bring to issues. The mere knowledge that our position is not the only position and may not be the right position leads us to ask questions in different ways with more openness and humility. On a more practical level, perhaps this humility can lead to greater collaboration across differences.

Restorative Love Economics

8

Hi, I'm Yaa Addae. Welcome to *Restorative Love Economics 101*, a meditation on transmitting care using the technology of imagination.

Find a comfortable position, one that allows you to hold yourself. If you can, lie down. I invite you to place your hands on your chest and close your eyes as we imagine counter-responses to ongoing structural violence.

8

What are you feeling in your body at this moment? Acknowledge the emotions and thoughts that are vying for your attention.

Breathe in for 3, and out. You have reached a portal. As you reach out towards the vastness in front of you, a wave of calm passes through your entire body.

You begin to lean in slowly, feeling relaxed and curious as you slip into a memory.

When was the last time you felt cared for?

Call forth this warmth and sink into it.

This year, I have been deeply moved by the following:

the bravery that authentic connection requires

loving my way towards a kinder future

design as an act of conjuring a world rooted in care

At the root of my creative practice is making space for others. This shows up in a number of ways and mediums in my work as a community researcher for a design studio, participatory curator, and writer. The focal point of my work has shifted over time from harnessing play towards authenticity, to encouraging the potential of imagination to create new visions of the world and, in this current moment, cultivating love as a balm against social alienation. For a feeling that has taken as many forms as the lives that have changed in its wake, love remains underexamined. There is much to be said about the ways in which modern capitalist society has designed slowness out of our lives, thus making checking in with ourselves a practice that has to be cultivated. bell hooks writes in *All About Love: New Visions* (arguably the foundation of Black feminist love studies), "To open our hearts more fully to love's power and grace we must dare to acknowledge how little we know of love in both theory and practice. [...] We yearn to end the lovelessness that is so pervasive in our society. This book tells us how to return to love." It was this thinking that spurred the origins of my ongoing experiential research programme, *Open Heart Clinic*. My heart is a compass I am still learning to follow, in my practice as a designer, and a continuous creator of my life.

Beyond aimless navel-gazing, this positive obsession with how we nurture one another is informed by a rigorous ethic of care that is necessary for our survival in a political landscape that is decidedly anti-love.

To turn our gaze towards those whom care has been directed away from—Black, queer, the working class—people, who have for centuries alchemised societal assaults on our being, is an act of resistance. If there is such a thing as structural violence, then there must be a possibility of structural love. Ultimately, design is a process of conjuring an idea into this realm and in doing so, making way for a set of behaviours.

Restorative Love Economics as a framework asks: what does it mean to redistribute love towards the systemically underloved?

For these past few months, I have been further meditating on these two questions:

How has systemic trauma transformed our capacities for intimacy?

What obstacles do systemically underloved communities face in loving and receiving love (familial, romantic, platonic, etc.)?

Inspired by Ntozake Shange's choreopoem *for colored girls who have considered suicide / when the rainbow is enuf*, by African indigenous healing rituals (or what Nigerian playwright and author Wole Soyinka calls the "drama of the gods"), and by my training as a facilitator of the Black Therapy Network's *Emotional Emancipation Circles*, I have a vested interest in exploring how systemic trauma transforms our interpersonal relationships and in probing the potential of design justice to hold space for reparative work.

To answer these questions, we must first:

1   RECOGNISE LOVELESSNESS
Part of addressing the need to counter structural violence with structural love is first attuning ourselves to the intricacies of lovelessness. When police surveillance is better funded than public health, that is anti-love. When the police are called into a classroom in the United Kingdom because a 15-year-old Black girl is 'suspected' of having weed on her instead of responding with concern, that is anti-love. When a government official suggests that people make more money in response to a cost of living crisis that has left an elderly woman riding the bus to stay warm, that is anti-love.

2   ARTICULATE A MORE SPECIFIC LANGUAGE FOR LOVE
Love, including its arteries, such as care, devotion and desire, for example, determines more than social capital and respect. It's a marker of who gets to live—and to live well. In the Yoruba religion, Ifa, earth is regarded as the marketplace where souls come to gain wisdom and experiences. Love, too, is a resource, one that is required in so many different ways that any

attempts to define it, such as the popular 'Love Languages' test, still don't articulate needs as well as they could. Restorative Love Economics requires asking people how they want to be loved outside of capitalist constraints and responding to those needs specifically.

3 RESTORING OUR CAPACITY FOR COLLECTIVE INTIMACY

Now where do we go from here? In her essay 'On the Issue of Roles', Toni Cade Bambara notes that "Revolution begins with the self, in the self. The individual, the basic revolutionary unit, must be purged of poison and lies that assault the ego and threaten the heart, that hazard the next larger unit—the couple or pair, that jeopardize the still larger unit—the family or cell, that put the entire movement in peril." Undoing systemic harm by moving forward with a framework of Restorative Love Economics is to heal the absence of care in social systems and restore our capacity for intimacy at scale through transforming ourselves.

Totems of social design:
A new politics of material culture

9

Industrial design differs from its sister arts of architecture and engineering in one basic way: it is the only profession that has moved from discovery to degeneracy in one generation. Members of the profession have lost integrity and responsibility and become purveyors of trivia, the tawdry and the shoddy, the inventors of toys for adults.—Victor J. Papanek (1971)

In the early 1970s, a ground-breaking book, provocatively titled *Design for the Real World: Human Ecology and Social Change*, emerged as a totem for a radical new genre of socially responsible design. Condensing within its pages an ersatz manifesto for an era facing the onset of post-industrial upheaval and environmental disaster, its prophetic warning "that industrial design, as we have come to know it, should cease to exist" holds even greater resonance today, in a world of unbridled disposability. Flanked on the activist-designer's bookshelf by Rachel Carson's warning of imminent ecological disaster, *Silent Spring* (1962), and Teresa Hayter's critique of the mechanisms of neo-colonialism, *Aid as Imperialism* (1971), it propelled its author, designer and critic Victor Papanek, to the apex of his career as the late twentieth century's agent provocateur of design.

As one of the most widely read and influential design books, translated into over twenty languages and never having fallen out of print since its inception, Design for the Real World converted a generation through its clarion call to embrace a fresh politics of design. Its legacy continues today, manifest in areas ranging from design anthropology, the maker movement, critical and inclusive design, and beyond. Pre-empting the twentiefirst century shift towards design as a dispersed transdisciplinary phenomenon, the polemic provoked uprisings within design schools through its critique of design's unspoken role in bolstering social inequality, ableism and discrimination by engendering cultural homogeneity with a 'one-size-fits-all' mentality. Instead, it proposed a humane design approach imbued with anthropological sensitivity to the local, the vernacular, and an understanding of the broader cultural nuances of design's power in undermining or solidifying social inclusion. In challenging design's assumed role as the originator of an ever-expanding field of products in an age of over-abundance, its overarching message was that design had the potential to be the key agent of social change, rather than a tool for stylisation, aestheticisation, or a driver for increased consumption. Ultimately, it advocated for a holistic model in which design is understood as inseparable from the social relations, customs, rituals and histories in which they are embedded.

Drawing on the cutting-edge social projects of students and previously little-known designers, its influence spanned North America, Europe, the Soviet Union, and the Global South. It prompted a revolution in design pedagogy by introducing a distinctly anthropological method into design practice that challenged the rational market logic of capitalism as the driver of innovation. At the forefront of its approach was the idea that users themselves should lie at the core of a radically new design practice that favoured vernacular and indigenous solutions rather than the technocratic ideologies of modernism. Despite being over a half-century old, it remains widely read in design schools across the world as a manifesto for change.

9

THE DESIGNER AS QUASI-ANTHROPOLOGIST

In 1973, the Italian edition of Papanek's polemic was released under the title *Progettare per il mondo reale. Il design: come è e come potrebbe essere* (Designing for the real world: how it is and how it could be). In January that same year, the seminal design magazine *Casabella* launched the radical open-ended pedagogic experiment *Global Tools* featuring leading figures of Italian radical design and architecture, from Archizoom Associati, Riccardo Dalisi, Gaetano Pesce, Ugo La Pietra, Ettore Sottsass through to Superstudio and U.F.O. The group espoused an exploratory, multi-disciplinary didactic series of workshops premised on generating an alternative culture of design, untethered from the legacy of Fordist industrial relations and conformist design school traditions. Just as Papanek's book lambasted the failure of contemporary design education for its emphasis on profits and 'clients' rather than an engagement with social needs, the Global Tools initiative revolved around a multi-sited 'anti-school' for design. Makers would be re-enchanted through engagement with pre-industrial craft-based genres, the sensorial process of design becoming a political strategy within itself.

Most importantly, Design for the Real World and Global Tools shared an agenda to reaffirm the social purpose of design beyond the rubric of modernism, offering fervent critiques of late industrial society's role in fostering widespread alienation and the destruction

9

While the radical Italian designers shared a similar set of objectives with the 'real world' agenda of socially responsible design, the release of the Italian edition of Design for the Real World also unleashed a fierce attack on its entire premise.

of local resources, indigenous knowledge, cultures, and skills. While Papanek's examples of the autochthon were mainly found in 'developing' countries and communities (including Greenland and Indonesia with Bali in particular), members of the Global Tools collective turned to the eroding peasant cultures of Italy, and more specifically Tuscany. Both Papanek and the radical Italian collective advocated multidisciplinary, experimental and non-hierarchical models of pedagogy and the dismantling of contemporary design conventions in favour of alternative economics of value. Using rhetoric that strikes a chord with designers in the early 21st century, they envisaged a devolved 'maker culture' rising from the ashes of the post-industrial, crisis-ridden late capitalism, that would empower localised groups, individuals and society. Original Global Tools member Franco Raggi described the project thus: "As opposed to the established and accepted practice of technological, comfortable, useful and functional design, the intent is to posit a nomadic practice for an archaic, dysfunctional design."[1] Anthropologically inspired ideas around material culture and ritual meaning, and an emphasis on users and co-design, underpinned their newly forged design philosophies.

9

THE POTENT OBJECT

One high-profile prototype that emerged from this new politics of design exemplified the contradictions of a movement that aimed to apply design to socially meaningful purposes, while seeking to distance itself from neo-colonial intervention.

The battery-free *Tin Can Radio* (designed by Victor Papanek and his student George Seeger for UNESCO) was powered with dried animal dung and constructed from waste components, intended for distribution among non-literate and isolated communities. Its image featured prominently on the dust jacket of the first edition of Design for the Real World, with the words of endorsement by Finnish designer Barbro Kulvik-Siltavuori pre-empting the criticism the design would come to provoke: "Today there is much controversy about design responsibility. Some think [Papanek] is too political, others that he is not political enough; some that he encourages neo-colonial exploitation, others that he is selling out the white race."

While the radical Italian designers shared a similar set of objectives with the 'real world' agenda of socially responsible design, the release of the Italian edition of Design for the Real World also unleashed a fierce attack on its entire premise. In the pages of *Casabella*, leading design theorist Gui Bonsiepe (alumnus of the Ulm School of Design) berated Papanek for his naïve and neo-colonial approach to socially responsible design. Bonsiepe condemned the social designers' attempts to address inequality through design as a "pale crusade of the petit bourgeois", criticizing the fact "that no mention is ever made of the organization of relationships of production and the role of productive forces, especially that of the working class". Referring to the much-fêted Tin Can Radio design for the 'Third World', the excoriating review implicated its designer in a broader conspiracy, that of working covertly for the US military: "The radio constitutes a tool of ideological penetration and control, and what drove the development of the project has now been transformed into nothing less than a tool of UNESCO pageantry." Bonsiepe hammered the last nail in the coffin of Papanek's radical and socially responsible design profile with the pointed comment that: "Maybe the author, during his stay in the USA and his attacks against the design 'establishment' thought he could find allies in military circles, a tactical, strategically disastrous error."

9   SOCIAL DESIGN: DISCONTENTS
          AND LEGACIES

The social design experiments and initiatives of the early 1970s, conceived outside the indices of purely commercial motives, were riddled with contradictions, many of which could be said to pertain to socially responsible design today.

And yet multiple aspects of that original social design agenda remain pertinent: the exploration of indigenous design, the critical appraisal of the role designers play in accelerating (and remedying) global climate change, and the pressing question of what form design's socio-environmental accountability might take. Moreover, design remains, as was claimed in the heyday of radical politics, a force as likely to inflict harm as to remedy it. Tasked with shaping our

material and immaterial existence, should designers be held answerable to broader humanitarian goals,
or merely to the whims of their techno-ideological
paymasters? Just how far does their responsibility extend to the long-term outcomes of their work, be it
a driverless vehicle or a disposable diaper? Although
the global application of much of today's social design is debatable, without the new political agenda of
the early 1970s, design would have remained a non-
critical, rationalised, problem solving and homogenous
practice—one that served only minority interests.

[1] Franco Raggi. 'Dysfunctional objects for a hereti-
cal "inverse ergonomics."' Notes of the Global
Tools seminar, 'The Body and Constraints', Milan,
1975.

9

Talk to me!
The Design Lab
at the Kunst-
gewerbemuseum
Berlin

10

The many museums of arts and crafts which were founded in Europe and North America in the late nineteenth century built on a vision of gigantic scope— nothing less than to guarantee product quality and educate the tastes of consumers. Most of the museums of arts and crafts also drew on an equally innovative concept: to build exemplary collections and to educate. This meant that museum and school were frequently found under one roof and thus merged as alternative places of learning. Museums of arts and crafts were far ahead of their time and, coincidentally, firmly rooted in the reality of daily life in the industrial age.

At the turn of the century, educating people's taste held a lot of practical potential, which was at the same time closely linked with economic interests. Proceeding from the existential question "How do we want to, or should we, live?", the great Art Nouveau reform project launched with no lesser ambition than to reform society through design, thus establishing a direct and critical connection between industrial production and private life.

The design pedagogies of the twentieth century reflect the evolution of society in an industrial nation that had subscribed to an unconditional belief in progress through technology, science and plannability, bolstered by ideas ranging from Walter Gropius's credo "Art and technology. A new unity" to the maxim of the Ulm School of Design, "Design is measurable". As design increasingly became a recognised and effective tool for the production of social reality, the social dimensions of design came into focus: from as early as the 1960s, the discipline per se came under intensifying criticism. Even in 2011, Lucy Kimbell asked, "Design leads us where exactly?" If design should fulfil an important social function, posited Kimbell, then which knowledge do design students need?

And the museums of arts and crafts? Where do they stand in the conflict situation roughly outlined above? In a nutshell, just a few decades after their stimulating foundation, they had passed the pinnacle of their powers. Not only did the schools of arts and crafts dissolve their institutional links with museums, but the term 'arts' also came to dominate. With this, the museums of arts and crafts changed direction. The industrial arts, and along with that every-

Today, the museum institution is on trial for many reasons. To some extent, this also applies to arts and crafts museums. They must work harder than other museums to prove their relevance, which they have progressively lost over recent decades. That said, they are far 'closer to life'; a critical examination of the production of things and the design of our lived-in worlds is to a degree embedded in their DNA.

10

thing this term implies in terms of theory and practice, were gradually pushed into the background. With Art Nouveau, which was celebrated with such pomp at the 1900 Paris Exposition, the majority of museums collected contemporary work for the last time in many years. Thereafter, contemporary design was primarily showcased in the new housing exhibitions or in other special exhibitions. In fact, up to the 1980s it was predominantly applied arts that found their way into the schools of arts and crafts, in Germany at least.[2] So-called product design is a relatively recent collection area and only made it onto the agenda of desirable objects some 40 years ago.

Today, the museum institution is on trial for many reasons. To some extent, this also applies to arts and crafts museums. They must work harder than other museums to prove their relevance, which they have progressively lost over recent decades. That said, they are far 'closer to life'; a critical examination of the production of things and the design of our lived-in worlds is to a degree embedded in their DNA. Meanwhile, numerous arts and crafts museums have set out on a path of fundamental change to refocus their agenda, in many cases returning to their founding impulse, now again highly relevant. This makes them attractive once again as alternative places of learning for students of all design disciplines and for artisans, who by the same token are rediscovering the potential of these museums.

To support this osmotic revitalisation process, in 2019 the *Design Lab* series was initiated at the

Kunstgewerbemuseum (Museum of Decorative Arts) of the Staatliche Museen zu Berlin. The series ran until 2022, in thirteen iterations. Conceived as a process-led project, the Design Lab was actualised in various formats ranging from an online research festival[3] and workshops[4] to an analogue exhibition and a digital reader. It utilised the multi-dimensional collections, which extend from the Middle Ages into the present day, as an archive, and combined the historical perspectives of this knowledge storage system with forward-looking design research. In our digital world, in which the haptic and material dimension increasingly escape us, the 'arts and crafts' collections in particular can act as catalysts for questions about the complex topic of design in the light of the imminent transformation of our living environments.

In the discourse on sustainability, materials play a critical role. Materials structure our society in political, economic, environmental, social and cultural terms. Materials form resources that wars were, and are, being fought over. Materials have been, and still are, root causes of colonisations. The geo- and biopolitical dynamics surrounding materials have highly critical effects on the environment, the climate and the social structures of local populations.

Museums of arts and crafts are also intrinsically archives of materials. From the aim of establishing an exemplary collection for all crafts practitioners and future designers evolved a systematisation of objects, adopted from the natural sciences, according to genre, geographical origin, and materiality. The main

Which objects are exhibited, and which stay in storage? Which classification criteria are collections and their presentation forms based on? How does an object become an exhibit? How do contextual shifts affect the understanding and impact of objects? Which histories are told in the classical presentation and which are not?

material groups included, first and foremost, textiles, metals, ceramics, glass and wood. The so-called modern materials, most notably plastics, were added to these.

Material was therefore a focal point of several Design Lab projects. Design Lab #5 'Times of Waste. The Leftover' focused on the transformation processes of a smartphone and investigated one of the world's most important technologies, which leaves behind many forms of waste, starting with the extraction of the raw materials it contains.[5] Design Lab #11 'LithoMania' focused on the positive and negative aspects of gemstones.[6] Design Lab #13 'Material Legacies' explored the unsustainable pasts and present of materials and conceptualised possible material future scenarios, focusing specifically on shape-shifting surfaces and phase-shifting textiles.[7]

With the term 'capitalocene', researchers endeavour to redefine the current age in which our capitalist forms of production and consumption radically affect all aspects of our geological, biological and atmospheric environment. One of the most important strategies to slow down these negative developments is circularity. Design Lab #8 'Material Loops. Paths to a Circular Future' presented a selection of forward-looking design projects ranging from best practice examples from industry to speculative experiments from design schools.[8] Places in Berlin engaging in circular practices were also introduced.

Design Lab #7 'Talk to Me! Consulting the Collections' focused on the critical reflection of the hegemonic prerogative of interpretation and knowledge discourses of arts and crafts museums given that they still predominantly reflect the collection strategies, systematisations and epistemologies of the nineteenth century.[9] Students working towards a Master of Arts in Art Education, Curatorial Studies at Zurich University of the Arts addressed questions such as, Who decides what is collected? Which criteria form a basis for collecting? Which objects are exhibited, and which stay in storage? Which classification criteria are collections and their presentation forms based on? In addition, they explored aspects of museum education, asking, How does an object become an exhibit? How do contextual shifts affect the understanding and impact of objects? Which histo-

10

ries are told in the classical presentation and which are not?

To make museum objects speak for themselves, to recognise them as echo chambers of the unseen, and to integrate them in a multi-perspective network of meanings are among the central tasks of museum education. At the same time, they present the greatest challenges with regard to reaching and appealing to a diverse audience. As a learning platform, the Design Lab thus also opens up a realm of possibilities for various actors, researchers, designers and students to reconsider museum and pedagogical practices and bring these into the contemporary discourse.

1   Lucy Kimbell. 'Design leads us where exactly?', Lecture from the symposium *Making Crafting Designing* at Schloss Solitude, Stuttgart, 2011. http://designleadership.blogspot.com/2011/03/making-crafting-designing-2011.html, accessed 3 October 2022.

2   The biggest exception is the *Neue Sammlung* (New Collection) in Munich, which, as the name implies, was founded in the 1920s as a collection of new design objects. https://dnstdm.de/sammlung/, accessed 3 October 2022.

3   Design Lab #6. '(How) do we (want to) work (together) (as (socially engaged) designers (students and neighbours)) (in neoliberal times)?' was originally planned as an analogue festival in the rooms of the Museum of Decorative Arts. Due to the Covid-19 pandemic, it took place in a digital space instead. https://www.smb.museum/museen-einrichtungen/kunstgewerbemuseum/ausstellungen/detail/design-lab-6/, accessed 25 September 2022. A book of the same name, edited by Claudia Banz and Jesko Fezer, was published by Sternberg Press.

10

4   Design Lab #2 'Less is Less—More is More. The Production of Everyday Life' was realised in cooperation with the *space&designSTRATEGIES* of the University of Arts Linz. A group of students explored the routines that both produce and characterise our daily lives. In a three-day workshop residency, they 'occupied' the museum as a research space full of 'objects disconnected from daily life'. https://www.smb.museum/museen-einrichtungen/kunstgewerbemuseum/ausstellungen/detail/design-lab-2/, accessed 25 September 2022.

5   The exhibition was curated by Flavia Caviezel and Mirjam Bürgin, who also directed the homonymous research project at the FHNW Academy of Art and Design, Basel. https://times-of-waste.ch/en/home-en/. An interdisciplinary symposium broadened and deepened the perspective on the waste narrative. http://times-of-waste.ch/en/symposium-en/, accessed 25 September 2022.

6   Design Lab #4 came about in cooperation with the Idar-Oberstein campus of Trier University of Applied Sciences. Cf. Claudia Banz, Ute Eitzenhöfer (eds.). *Lithomania*. Stuttgart: Arnold'sche, 2021. https://www.smb.museum/museen-einrichtungen/kunstgewerbemuseum/ausstellungen/detail/design-lab-11/, accessed 25 September 2022.

7   Design Lab #13 presented research findings from diverse contributors to the excellence cluster Matters of Activity and was curated by Emile de Visscher and Michaela Büsse. https://www.smb.museum/museen-einrichtungen/kunstgewerbemuseum/ausstellungen/detail/design-lab-13/, accessed 25 September 2022.

8   For Design Lab #8, the curatorial team of the Museum of Decorative Arts cooperated with the Hans Sauer Stiftung in Munich, which prioritises research into and funding for social design and, in this context, focuses sharply on the target vision of a recycling society (https://www.hans-sauerstiftung.de/themen/). Participants of the Recò

10

Festival on circular practice founded in 2019 in Prato were also invited as special guests. https://www.recofestival.it/. A digital reader was also published to coincide with Design Lab #8. Edited by Claudia Banz, Barbara Lersch and Kaja Ninnis, this may be downloaded at https://smart.smb.museum/media/exhibition/73498/Reader_DesignLab-8_Web.pdf, accessed 28 May 2023.

9   Due to the pandemic, it was not possible to hold the exhibition. The format was therefore transformed into an online poster exhibition, which may be downloaded at https://blog.zhdk.ch/design-lab7/. The research findings were published in an homonymous magalog which was edited by Claudia Banz and Angeli Sachs. https://www.smb.museum/museen-einrichtungen/kunstgewerbemuseum/ausstellungen/detail/design-lab-7/, accessed 25 September 2022.

10

Termokiss: Fighting old policies with new practices in Prishtina

Termokiss is a community-run centre in Kosovo's capital city, Prishtina, with the mission of urban and civil exchange, reflection and changemaking. Based on a once derelict site, it has become a vibrant social and cultural hub, a safe space where people of all backgrounds and ages can meet, work and learn together, and an ever-evolving model for grassroots social design—all thanks to a collective of creative young people.

Termokiss was born in 2016 in reaction to the waves of privatisation of public and socially owned spaces and enterprises imposed on Kosovo after the war in 1999. Under the neoliberal policies pursued under the administration of the UN Mission in Kosovo (UNMIK), vast numbers of ex-factories, properties and facilities were handed over to local and international private businesses and corporations in the hope of economic rebirth. Yet the supposed trickle-down effect has repeatedly proven to be a farce. As economist and political scientist Rita Augestad Knudsen's extensive research on the early stages of the privatisation process shows, out of the hundreds of people she interviewed, not a single main actor was able to offer an alternative solution to accelerated privatisation at that time. But that is changing. Younger generations in Kosovo have been coming up with new initiatives to reclaim public space. Termokiss is one of them.

Prishtina's pioneering community centre was initiated by Toestand, a Belgian NGO specialised in reappropriating abandoned buildings, and brought to life with the help of a handful of people from Kosovo. Established first as a squat, Termokiss was built in a former facility of the city heating company, Termokos. Its community consisted of people of different backgrounds trying to grapple with the idea of public space. For a short period, the space functioned without permission. Later on, the use of the space was approved by the municipality of Prishtina, camouflaged as a "special decision". Despite the precedent set by Termokiss, no legal framework has been established to allow for other such transformations of public space.

In the first six months of its existence, the Termokiss community organised more than 600 activities (music events, training sessions, movie screenings, etc.). Such initiatives reflect the hunger of the younger generations for a new approach, for spaces where community members can express themselves freely and open up new ways of making and exhibiting art, sharing knowledge and education, and creating different levels of consciousness and awareness of their surroundings.

The community laid the groundwork for the centre's structure and decision-making processes within the first few weeks. Inspired by alternative decision-making models, Termokiss has established strictly horizontal decision-making practices in the community. There is no hierarchy; decisions are taken during weekly meetings, held on Wednesdays, on the principle of 'one member, one vote'. The tradition of Wednesday meetings has continued ever since the very beginning of Termokiss six years ago. The calls to attend these meetings are made verbally as well as through emails and social media groups and platforms.

This structure of decision-making was entirely derived from the ongoing activities happening in the space. As the number of activities organised by the community rose, the space began to gather more and more people around it. The sense of cohesion grew consistently, thus paving the way to flesh out the decision-making process and exposing the need for principles that would serve as pillars of the community and the space.

The community consists of its members and the staff that maintain the space, who, as with any other important decision, are elected in the weekly meetings. The staff members are equal to any other member, but they also carry the responsibilities of coordinating and leading the project from which their income is generated.

The principles of Termokiss were established in a long and open process, in which community members would negotiate for hours on matters of wording, inclusivity, boundaries (no boundaries), activities and functionality. Of all the principles adhered to, the two that thrive the most are those of intergenerational sharing and inclusivity.

The principle of intergenerational sharing calls for leading staff to hand over their position to newer members every two years so they might claim those positions and gain experience in working in such

11

spaces and conditions. Since they are likely to be the members who spend the most time at the space, they have the possibility to navigate towards the ideas which they embrace, bringing about different approaches and priorities for the community.

The principle of inclusivity states that everybody is welcome at Termokiss, but this principle also relies on the agreements reached in the weekly meetings and the individuals who visit the space. There are clear limits to this principle. Inclusion doesn't extend to any individual who holds supremacist beliefs, is violent in any form, disturbs the activities going on in the space or engages in any other actions that collide with the centre's principles and regulations.

Inspired by alternative decision-making models, Termokiss has established strictly horizontal decision-making practices in the community.

11

The grassroots manner in which these principles were established reflects the processes, activities and work taking place in the space, and harmonise directly with the framework which evolved within the community.

The importance of this process is supported by the research of Elinor Ostrom, who was awarded the Nobel Prize for Economics. In her book *Governing the Commons: The Evolution of Institutions for Collective Action,* she clearly states that communities maintaining and using a space together have a bigger chance of failing if they lack clear principles.

INITIATIVES AND ACHIEVEMENTS IN THE COMMON STRUGGLE FOR PUBLIC SPACE

The establishment of the community through activities and exchanges with different non-governmental organisations gave rise to a common struggle for public space. In 2017, the Termokiss community joined forces with different NGOs and individuals from all over Kosovo to launch the initiative *Mundësi për Krejt* (Opportunity for All). The main purpose of this initiative was to initiate a change in the law that governs the allocation for use and exchange of municipal immovable property. The main concerns at that time included the monopolist power wielded by corporations and businesses in laying claim to public spaces owned by the municipality of Prishtina, and the lack of a legal framework that would enable NGOs and initiatives to lay claim to such spaces.

The lack of transparency was seen in a similarly critical light as was the law stating that business and market activity alone serve the common (public) good. Hence, the new alliance of NGOs started a petition to change that law. It was signed by thousands of people who shared the same struggle or who supported the idea that citizens should have the right to lay claim to abandoned spaces.

In April 2019, the new law governing the allocation for use and exchange of municipal immovable property came into effect. Even though not all the recommendations were passed into law, the most important article was the one deeming civil initiatives and NGOs to be legal subjects in possession of the right to claim municipal property. This opened up new dimensions for the use of public spaces and provided a legal basis for future activities in this field. The new law offers transparency when it comes to identifying and claiming spaces for public use. It obliges the municipality to disclose every property it owns and any plans it has affecting the present or future of that property.

The success of this initiative cast a very different light on public spaces and their usage and transformation. It not only made people aware of the existence of such spaces and the possibilities they offer, but also created a new participatory political discourse and sense of empowerment upon which future projects and initiatives could build.

Termokiss is no longer a novelty, but an integral part of daily life. It has made people believe that sustainable and safe social and community spaces can—and should—continue to exist.

COMMUNITY SPACE AS COMMUNITY GRACE

The broad range of community-derived projects frequently manifest themselves in the form of clubs. In fact, from the very beginning the formation of clubs such as the neighbourhood club, the juggling club, music clubs and the video club have played a central role in building a community around Termokiss. Club meetings and activities have brought a huge amount of people to the centre. This growing involvement has created a very healthy social cohesion within the community, which has also shaped the way the space is used.

The community has given rise to numerous other initiatives, some of which have established themselves so well that they have formed their own NGOs.

One example is *Bukë për Krejt* (Bread for all). What started off as an idea to find ways of distributing food to people in need has meanwhile evolved into a large-scale initiative. Supported by many activists, the organisation distributes food to people in need on a daily and weekly basis. It is one of the leading initiatives to have grown from the Termokiss community.

Another example is a recently created collective whose name roughly translates as 'The name comes last'. The collective is currently operating in the city of Fushë Kosova with members who were and still are part of the Termokiss community. Located just ten kilometres away from Prishtina, Fushë Kosova is a small town with a diverse profile. It is home to Albanian, Serbian and Roma communities. The main idea is to 'pass the torch', as it were, to share the tools developed by Termokiss to reuse and rebuild abandoned spaces in Fushë Kosova. The idea is to create a community and, in so doing, to raise awareness for the potential of the communal—as opposed to business and corporate—usage of abandoned buildings and properties. At the same time, the collective aims to demonstrate that it is not only around big cities that this kind of initiative can work.

Like other ongoing initiatives, these two projects clearly reflect the community's strong opposition of capitalist values and its powerful commitment to creating alternative methods of distributing knowledge, ideas and goods to all people, regardless of their backgrounds and means.

The Termokiss community applies to different funding bodies, both local and international, some of which can be institutional. Project applications are written and submitted in close conversation with the members of the community and depend very much on the necessities at any given time. Funding varies according to the public's needs. These are discussed within the community project, leading to future plans for investments, infrastructure and tools.

Termokiss is run from a building measuring 300 square metres with a garden around it. The space is thus a very important resource, guaranteeing the community's ongoing activities. The community tries to make as much use as possible of its size and scope. Renting the space out is another way to generate income. The fee for using the space is not always levied. Indeed, it is often waived for young initiatives, NGOs or local music groups. But institutions, international organisations and well-funded organisations are obliged to pay a fee and thus contribute directly to the funds of the space and the community.

In recent years, the garden has also been transformed into a source of self-sustainability. Operating as an urban garden, its produce is harvested and used by the community. Very often it is also used by the *Bukë për Krejt* initiative to help provide food packages to people in need.

Ultimately, all initiatives using public spaces in similar ways share the same struggle of remaining financially independent, in Kosovo as in many other

11

places around the region. There is a shortage of funding sources compatible with the community's value system. While this makes it harder to keep things running, it also challenges the community to come up with new methods and ideas about how to raise and use funds.

After six years of existence, Termokiss is no longer a novelty, but an integral part of daily life. It has made people believe that sustainable and safe social and community spaces can—and should— continue to exist. Even state institutions have come to recognise the value of this kind of initiative. Many of their representatives have grown to respect the ideas such initiatives represent and explore, and to look to the innovative ways in which they have shown community spaces can be used and can contribute to the social fabric. Besides the successful change to the law, Termokiss and other such initiatives have helped not only to create a platform for reclaiming public spaces, but also to build a bridge between people and institutions so that they might work together to define the future of the spaces at hand.

11

Never get too comfortable: On schooling design

12

CATHERINE NICHOLS Dear Marina, it was the productive disquiet with which you work on design institutions *within* design institutions that first caught my attention. It was your restless quest to rethink, to re-imagine, to co-think, to co-imagine institutional paradigms and design pedagogies that drew me deeper into your research, that made me want to listen to your presentations and somehow retrace the trajectory of the thought process that has brought you to where you are now: at the forefront of reflection on how design practices and practitioners might rise to the social, economic, political and ecological challenges we face on a planetary scale.

In registering your preoccupation with temporal, itinerant structures and sites of learning, already manifest in your doctoral thesis *Evanescent Institutions: Political Implications of an Itinerant Architecture* (2016), I was reminded of an idea I stumbled across some years ago in conducting research on Black Mountain College as an exemplar of ideal or alternative universities. John Andrew Rice, the college's founding rector, argued that colleges should be in tents. Rice was convinced that any idea, no matter how humane, no matter how progressively-minded, would sink into the institution within ten years, at which point the college could—and should—fold up like a tent and move on, regroup, think again. Looking at the history of design education, do you think there's something to be said for Rice's tent theory? Might the 'tent', whether physical or metaphorical, be considered a prerequisite for innovation in design education?

MARINA OTERO VERZIER Thank you, Catherine, for your generous words and for taking the time to learn more about the work I do. Responding to your question: absolutely. It reminds me of a few projects that sparked my imagination for decades, that were case studies in my PhD thesis and always present during my attempts to study and test alternative institutional formations: *Misiones Pedagógicas* (Spain, 1931–1936) and *Laboratorio di Quartiere— Urban Travelling Reconstruction Workshop* by Renzo Piano (Otranto, Italy, 1979).

Whereas ephemerality is usually associated with instability, temporal projects (such as the aforementioned examples) could harvest enduring energy and transformations. Institutions and the people making them should not get too comfortable, to the point that processes, methods and aims are taken for granted. To remain relevant to society, institutions must be persistently reinvented and challenged from within—reflecting on and questioning their own practices, biases, structures, and the networks in which they operate. This strategy allows them to resist the temptation of relying only on known paths and validated trajectories.

To allow for emergent models, institutions must learn to channel disruptive powers of imagination. That means that sometimes they have to find a way to do the groundwork and evolve or, as Rice proposes, to fold up, move on, regroup, and think again. It is critical to recognise when an institution and those who represent it are driven by inertia, have become too entrenched in power, and are more concerned with its reputation and continuation than its relevance.

After more than seven years, I left my position at *Het Nieuwe Instituut* (HNI) to avoid becoming part of that type of institution. I had to redirect my commitment towards something more relevant than any single institution or myself and my career. It was not an easy decision or process. My main focus now is to make friends, comrades and allies, and to put together 'tents' for knowledge exchange, forms of solidarity, empathy and appropriate redistribution strategies while enjoying the time together. I am full of enthusiasm.

CN What about economic and political upheaval. Would you say that they were equally important motors for pedagogical innovation?

MOV Innovative approaches have emerged out of necessity and amid the turmoil of a global pandemic, recession, rising inequality and protests over racial injustice. Institutions, faced with societal demands against patriarchal and racial oppression and for more horizontal structures and power/knowledge relations, have embraced different strategies. At the core of the struggle is the future of living together. These actions and efforts held up a mirror to existing cultural institutions and those like me who worked in them. Some responded to the calls for their transformation and have carried out incomplete, contested, and,

At the core of the struggle is the future
of living together.

at times, failed yet relevant attempts at alternative
forms of organisation and action. Others made cos-
metic changes and focused on promoting the illusion
of stability.

In my work, I have analysed these processes and
made comparative studies with events that unfolded ten years ago. Then, unemployment, evictions, and
foreclosures resulted from the global economic recession that marked 2011, paving the way for growing
global unrest that manifested in anti-government
and anti-austerity protests calling for a 'real democracy'. At that moment, major museums and educational institutions launched initiatives that captured that
democratic movement and the interest in turning
cultural institutions into sociopolitical agencies (by

relocating cultural practices from the interior of institutions to urban public spaces). Examples include the Centre Pompidou Mobile, the BMW Guggenheim Lab or Studio-X.

Many institutions used temporal and mobile approaches to test new models and channel efforts to mitigate the institutionalised violence embedded in their existing structures. My research revealed that as the high walls of cultural institutions seemed to be dismantled, other borders emerged, perpetuating inclusion and exclusion conditions. Despite the innovations and significant transformations triggered by these and other institutions, they also turned into mechanisms of social order and part of urban gentrification processes. Once carrying a subversive potential, the temporary structures were aligned with neoliberal dynamics and were ultimately affected (and put to an end) by the volatility of the markets they served.

These episodes reflected critically on my experience of studying and testing alternative formations—decentralised models for universities, itinerant museums and more-than-human cooperatives.

CN ▮ Looking at the way you and your colleagues developed the research programme at Het Nieuwe Instituut, the Netherlands' national museum for architecture, design and digital culture founded in 2013, I found the dedication to developing regenerative strategies within one and the same institution striking and inspiring. I guess you could think of it as an ongoing pitching and dismantling of tents. *Neuhaus*, a temporary academy seeking to reactivate the founding spirit of Bauhaus 100 years on, might be thought of as one such tent. Could you please tell us a little bit about the objectives of this reactivation in 2019? Which aspects of the Bauhaus pedagogy did you pick up, which did you reject and how did you and your many collaborators go about exploring, critiquing, expanding and transforming the concepts adopted by exponents of the Bauhaus?

MOV You put it beautifully. The ethos of the research team I directed at HNI was never to get too comfortable with our practices, methods, or ideas. We were interested in durational collective research processes instead of quick and stand-alone projects because they allowed us to establish and commit to meaningful alliances during the research. Long, open-ended processes also challenged some of our initial hypotheses and positions. And we discussed that in public, making ourselves vulnerable by showing the process of learning and unlearning, steps and missteps, accepting the possibility of oversights, and making them available for public scrutiny. This open nature didn't prevent the materialisation of ideas in concrete projects. Yet our projects were never fully finished, not even when they materialised in exhibitions or books. We would not wait until we figured everything out to open for public debate. Instead, our processes emphasised the commitment to sharing ideas and instigating public discussion in the face of the forms of value creation and knowledge fencing that have permeated educational and cultural institutions.

The same applies to the body of the institution and its workings. For us, the institution should host within it its possible alternative futures. In 2020, we even launched an open call titled *Regeneration: Open Call for New Institutions*. We imagined HNI as a testing ground for generative endeavours to test and rehearse new notions of the institution and 'instituting'. Proto-institutions that served as blueprints and route maps to interrogate the relevance of today's cultural infrastructures, starting from HNI, will eventually render them obsolete. It was a process of ongoing institutional ruination and emergence. It kept us busy!

Neuhaus was part of this trajectory, the idea of temporarily transforming the institution into something else, in this case, an academy for other knowledges. But I would argue that the project's idea came more from a sense of opportunism and a marketing strategy—to celebrate the anniversary of the Bauhaus and align HNI's program with the international conversation that occurred around this anniversary—and that limited its full potential. In the end, the history of the Bauhaus mainly became a trigger for something else. Even if opportunist, it unleashed dynamic and generative systems. It allowed the channelling of ideas, methods and tactics from generation to generation to assess their societal relevance.

CN   For me as an onlooker, one of the most captivating updates to the objectives set out by Walter

Gropius in his 1919 manifesto was the shift towards a more-than-human subjectivity…

MOV The relationships between human and nonhuman bodies, as well as their classification, have long been a site of inquiry for disciplines such as philosophy, geography, animal studies and radical social sciences. Whereas human/nonhuman ethics are at the centre of contemporary conversations on issues of inequality and the climate emergency, the discipline of architecture has been only timidly thinking beyond the centrality of the human subject. Architectural practices have primarily developed around normative constructions of the 'human' (and in particular the notion of 'man' as a universal, rational subject), and yet, they are entangled in non-anthropocentric struggles. They have a role in how encounters between beings are structured in time and space, but are generally orchestrated to serve the comfort and privilege of some humans.

The shift towards a more-than-human perspective allows the discipline to venture beyond its Cartesian postulates, prompting its critical reinvention. It unleashes other forms of relationality beyond the compartmentalisation and instrumentalisation of relations and exploitative and extractivist dynamics. It is fundamental for dismantling the boundaries for compassion and the borders that currently define, protect and exploit the common world. More-than-human thinking, I'd argue, dismisses the architecture centred around the white humanist masculinist subject who sees the world as his own possession.

CN   So, the idea of *zoöps* came about prior to the foundation of Neuhaus? Where has this line of questioning taken the institution—and you?

MOV The zoöps are one type of the testing grounds that we imagined would start as "just an experiment or a pilot project". The word zoöps is a combination of the Dutch word for 'cooperation', and 'zoë', Greek for 'life'. We used this jargon as a Trojan horse to allow disruption inside the institution under the lens of a temporary project. Still, our aim was that these initiatives could eventually transform or even take over the entire institution. These alternative institutions, we imagined, were operating platforms from which to put spatial, material, socioecological and conceptual models in motion, leading to paradigm shifts.

Influenced by the contemporary milieu characterised by the climate catastrophe, struggles for racial justice, and rising inequality (struggles institutions have often failed to support meaningfully), some of us questioned our positionality. Is it possible to practice alternative, better-suited institutions by working with and from the ruins of the existing and previous ones? Could existing structures be reshaped as non-exploitative spaces for the public good? What if these testing grounds are our main focus and not a disruptive force inside an existing institution? What if we thoroughly practis these alternative institutional formations, forms of gathering and engaging, without having to simultaneously be representatives of the very structures we aim to challenge? I realised, as did some of my colleagues and peers, that we had to continue the work outside the institution.

CN   I noticed that you have looked not only towards more-than-human subjects as sources of regenerative processes and practices in design learning but also to many different institutional paradigms. Which do you think have the most potential for imagining alternative futures?

MOV I have always tried to experiment with methodologies and forms of institutional practice to foster reciprocal relations between the public initiatives of an institution and its institutional culture. I wasn't always successful. Most of the time, I found myself in paradoxical positions, from which I nevertheless learned.

Still, I think some projects, such as those of the Oslo Architecture Triennale 2016 *After Belonging* (notably *The Academy* and the *New World Embassy: Rojava*) and HNI's archival intervention *Architecture of Appropriation* were able to unleash significant transformations. At the Royal College of Art, together with Kamil Dalkir and Ippolito Pestellini, we run the studio *Data Matter: Digital Networks, Data Centres & Posthuman Institutions*, which looked at the architecture of data centres as the testing ground for alternative models of post-human institutions. I continue reimagining these digital infrastructures and institutions with the support of Harvard's Wheelwright Prize.

With the zoöp and similar initiatives such as *Burn Out* and *Lithium: States of Extraction*, we tried to put in motion an environmentally conscious practice that could bring ecological thinking into everyday life. In so doing, we also wanted to acknowledge the intimate relationship between the current production and labour systems and burnout processes, with ongoing environmental exploitation and extraction. This is something I continue pursuing as head of the MA in Social Design at the Design Academy Eindhoven. There, we mobilise (not without struggle) design's capacity toward post-patriarchal, post-anthropocentric, ecological and plural forms of conviviality. We borrow from epistemologies of the South practices such as *Disoñar* (a neologism that merges 'design' with 'dream' coined by cultural activist and designer León Octavio Osorno in the mid-1980s and now used by several groups of peasant activists and intellectuals in Latin America to describe the actions of people who take responsibility for designing their dreams and executing them), or *Buen Vivir* (a decolonial stance that, according to its leading proponent Eduardo Gudynas, calls for new ethics that balance quality of life and the democratisation of the state).

These projects have sparked imaginations, and that is highly necessary. While other paradigms for facing ecological and social challenges are urgently needed, too many of us have lost our ability to imagine alternative worlds under current conditions. Today's tragedy is humanity's incapacity to imagine alternative futures. We are subjected to an appalling sense of exhaustion and finitude. Therefore, the exercise of the imagination is necessary to counter the various effects of defuturing (a term coined by design theorist Tony Fry) and the slow cancellation of the future (as argued by author Mark Fisher) of capitalist patriarchal modernity and its structural unsustainability. These defuturing processes, epitomised in modes of living, labouring, producing and consuming, have created a world that eliminates possible futures for humans and non-humans.

Recognising these tendencies, I decided to change gears before I fell into inertia. I am soon moving back to my country, Spain, and hope to organise a new 'tent' in the Galician mountains. The history of the place is intertwined with the regional legends, local ecosocial and feminist traditions of witchcraft, and spiritual practices associated with *El Camino de Santiago*, which has attracted millions of pilgrims for centuries. From there, I hope to embrace other ways of living, learning, working and caring. These might be incipient and clumsy, but they are also no longer postponable.

REGINA BITTNER

p. 9 Regina Bittner is head of the Academy and deputy director of the Bauhaus Dessau Foundation. She is responsible for the conception and teaching of the postgraduate programmes for design, Bauhaus and architecture research. She curated numerous exhibitions on the Bauhaus and the cultural history of modernism. Her main areas of work include: international architectural and urban research, modernism and migration, the cultural history of modernism, and heritage studies. The results of her research and teaching have been widely published. She studied cultural studies and art history at the University of Leipzig and completed her PhD at the Institute for European Ethnology at the Humboldt-Universität zu Berlin. Since 2019, she has been an honorary professor at the Institute for European Art History and Archaeologies at Martin Luther University Halle-Wittenberg.

13

CATHERINE NICHOLS

p. 17 Catherine Nichols is an arts and literary scholar, curator and writer based in Berlin. Since completing her doctorate at the University of New South Wales in Sydney, Australia, in 2001 with a thesis on Hans Magnus Enzensberger, she has curated a broad range of cultural history exhibitions at institutions across Germany on topics spanning from the Reformation to the passions, from the sun to sexuality. She has also mounted numerous monographic and thematic art exhibitions including *Beuys: We are the Revolution*, *The End of the 20th Century: The Best Is Yet to Come* and *Capital: Debt— Territory—Utopia* for the Nationalgalerie im Hamburger Bahnhof—Museum für Gegenwart—Berlin (in collaboration with Eugen Blume) and *Everyone is an Artist: Cosmopolitical Exercises with Joseph Beuys* (in collaboration with Isabelle Malz and Eugen Blume) at K20 Kunstsammlung Nordrhein-Westfalen in Düsseldorf. She has published widely on contemporary art as well as editing numerous catalogues and books, such as *Bruce Nauman: Ein Lesebuch*, *Black Mountain: An Interdisciplinary Experiment, 1933–1957*, and *Shine on Me: Wir und die Sonne*. She was the artistic director of *beuys 2021*, a year-long centenary programme comprising some 30 cultural events in the state of North Rhine-Westphalia as well as an online radio station, a symposium and an interdisciplinary laboratory exploring radical democratic forms of collectivity. She recently curated Manifesta 14 Prishtina—*it matters what worlds world worlds: how to tell stories otherwise*—and currently works as a curator at the Nationalgalerie im Hamburger Bahnhof—Museum für Gegenwart—Berlin.

KLÁRA PREŠNAJDEROVÁ

13

p. 29   Klára Prešnajderová (b. 1981) gained a degree in literary studies. Since 2018, she has been working as a research associate, an administrator of the archive of the School of Arts and Crafts, Bratislava and a curator at the Slovak Design Centre. Her research areas include art journals of the interwar period, modern typography, and the reform of art and arts and crafts education in Slovakia. She is the editor (with Simona Bérešová and Sonia de Puineuf) of the publications *School as a Laboratory of Modern Life. On the reform of art education in Central Europe (1900–1945)* and *ŠUR. Škola umeleckých remesiel v Bratislava 1928–1939* (ŠUR. School of Arts and Crafts in Bratislava 1928–1939).

SHANNAN CLARK

p. 41   Shannan Clark holds a doctorate in history and teaches a range of courses on the history of the modern United States. Prior to joining Montclair State in 2008, he taught at Tulane University, the University of Missouri at St. Louis, Columbia University, the Van Arsdale Labor Center of Empire State College (SUNY), and Princeton University. His research explores the development of white-collar work in the twentieth-century United States, with a particular focus on labour relations within the culture industries, including advertising, the print media, the broadcast media, and design. He is the author of *The Making of the American Creative Class: New York's Culture Workers and Twentieth-Century Consumer Capitalism.*

MARTIN MÄNTELE

p. 49   Martin Mäntele (b. 1965 in Meßkirch, Germany) has been head of the HfG Archive since 2013. He studied art history and modern German literature in Tübingen, Newcastle (GB) and Hamburg from 1984. In 1999, he completed his doctorate at the University of Tübingen. He is involved in numerous exhibition and publication projects. Since 2003, he has repeatedly taught design history at the universities of Ulm, Würzburg, Schwäbisch Gmünd, and Biberach.

ILANA S. TSCHIPTSCHIN

p. 65 Ilana S. Tschiptschin is a Brazilian researcher and graphic designer currently based in Berlin. She holds an MSc in Architecture and Urbanism from the São Paulo University (FAU-USP) and an MSc in Design Research from the Anhalt School of Applied Arts and the Humboldt Universität zu Berlin in cooperation with the Bauhaus Dessau Foundation. Her most recent research revolves around the entanglements between Brazilian and German post-war modern movements in art, design and architecture, questioning the flow between centre and periphery.

LESLEY-ANN NOEL

p. 75 Lesley-Ann Noel is an assistant professor in the Department of Design Studies at North Carolina State University. She has a BA in Industrial Design from the Universidade Federal do Paraná in Curitiba, Brazil, and a Master's degree in Business Administration from the University of the West Indies in Trinidad and Tobago. She earned her PhD in Design from North Carolina State University in 2018. She is co-Chair of the *Pluriversal Design Special Interest Group* of the Design Research Society. Before joining North Carolina State University, she was the Associate Director of *Design Thinking for Social Impact* at Tulane University in New Orleans, and a lecturer at Stanford University and the University of the West Indies. In her research, she promotes greater critical awareness among designers and design students by introducing critical theory concepts and vocabulary into the design studio, for example using *The Designer's Critical Alphabet* and the *Positionality Wheel.* She is one of the editors of *The Black Experience in Design*, an anthology featuring the stories of 70 Black designers, and is currently completing a book on design for social change.

YAA ADDAE

p. 87 Yaa Addae is a curator, writer and artist who works as a community researcher at the design agency COMUZI. Their practice is informed by the liberating power of the imagination, play, and restorative love economics, bringing love to the systemically underloved. Currently based between London and Accra, Yaa is a culture staff writer at the pan-African platform for women AMAKA and manages a digital studio, A-kra, which offers an online art history platform *(Decolonize The Art World)* and virtual residency programme *(The Imaginarium)*. They have spoken at the Southbank Centre (London), the Nubuke Foundation (Accra), the Barbican, and lead workshops with organisations like Autograph ABP, the Church of Black Feminist Thought, the Library of Africa and The African Diaspora, and Rumpus Room. In conjunction with the Gallery 31 exhibition *Swimmers Limb*, Yaa Addae is currently leading a workshop on cultivating future care infrastructures at Somerset House in London.

ALISON J. CLARKE

p. 95 Alison J. Clarke is a design historian (RCA/V&A) and a trained social anthropologist (UCL). She joined the University of Applied Arts Vienna as chair of design history and theory having previously held a senior faculty post at the Royal College of Art, London. Her most recent monograph, *Victor Papanek: Design for the Real World* (MIT Press, 2021) offers a critical perspective on the rise of the social design movement and the shift towards transdisciplinary design research. Clarke's approach uniquely combines historical and anthropological methodology, placing her work at the forefront of design anthropology research and of early debates within material culture, design and consumption studies. Her monograph *Tupperware: The Promise of Plastic in 1950s America* (Smithsonian Press, 2014) charted the inception and reception of an everyday design technology in the context of the ethnic and gendered social relations of postwar US culture and became the basis for an Emmy Award-nominated documentary. Other recent publications include the anthology *Design Anthropology: Object Cultures in Transition* (2017) and the co-edited volumes *Émigré Cultures in Design and Architecture* (2017) with E. Shapira, and *International Design Organizations: Histories, Legacies, Values* (2021) with J. Aynsley and T. Messell. Her latest book project explores the historical intersection of design and social science. As director of the Victor J. Papanek Foundation, Clarke heads the biennial symposia in contemporary design theory and recently initiated and co-curated, with the Vitra Design Museum, the international travelling exhibition *Victor Papanek: The Politics of Design*, and co-edited the accompanying exhibition catalogue. She has supervised design and material culture lectures at undergraduate and postgraduate level for over twenty-five years, previous students having taken up major roles in curatorship, academia and design practice. She is a recipient of a numerous competitive fellowships and awards (Smithsonian, Hagley/Winterthur, the Graham Foundation, USA; Arts and Humanities Research Council, UK) and has led several major international research projects, most recently *Émigré Cultural Networks and the Founding of Social Design* funded by the Austrian Science Fund (FWF). She is co-founder (with Victor Buchli, UCL) of *Home Cultures: Architecture, Design and Domestic Space* and editorial advisory board member of *Design and Culture*, the *Journal of Consumer Culture*, and *Material World* (NYU), regularly acting as a panel member on international academic research juries and external doctoral committees. She was recently awarded an Honorary Doctorate from the University of Southern Denmark in recognition of her research in the area of design and anthropology and is expert advisor to the Royal Danish Academy research project *Spaces of Danish Welfare*. She contributes regularly to a range of international media including the award-winning BBC television series *The Genius of Design*.

CLAUDIA BANZ

p. 105 Claudia Banz is an art and design expert, exhibition organiser and author. Since 2017, she has been curator of design at the Kunstgewerbemuseum (Museum of Decorative Arts), Berlin. Prior to that, Claudia Banz was a freelance curator and, from 2011 to 2017, head of the art and design department at the Museum für Kunst und Gewerbe Hamburg (Museum of Art and Design Hamburg). Banz has realised a number of well-regarded exhibitions, outreach projects and trade shows at the interface of design, fashion, art and crafts, including *Fast Fashion. Die Schattenseite der Mode*, *Food Revolution 5.0. Gestaltung für die Gesellschaft von morgen*, *Connecting Afro Futures. Fashion x Hair x Design* and *Retrotopia. Design for Socialist Spaces*. For the Kunstgewerbemuseum Berlin she

established the series *Design Lab* and *Design Talks,* designed
to open up the museum as a platform and experimental
space for multidisciplinary design approaches and a critical
discourse on socially relevant design issues. Banz is a
member of several juries, and her publications cover aspects
of social design, material culture and decolonial collections.

13 **ORBIS REXHA**

p. 117 Orbis Rexha is a jurist with a bachelor's degree in Law from
the University of Prishtina. As a researcher, activist and
law practitioner, he was involved in writing and publishing the
research project *Spaces of Commoning: Urban Commons
in the Ex-Yu Region.* Moreover, he has acted as a legal repre-
sentative of Termokiss at the Ministry of Local Government
Administration. He was part of the consultation process that
led to changes to the law that regulates public spaces in Kosovo, representing community needs for public spaces in the
interests of a fairer, non-commercial and more transparent
law. He has worked in the civil division of the Basic Court of
Prishtina assisting with legal tasks such as decisions and
verdicts, administrative processes, and monitoring legal processes. He has recently begun to work in the fields of environmental issues, public space, and mental health.

MARINA OTERO VERZIER

p. 129 Marina Otero Verzier is head of the Social Design master programme at the Design Academy Eindhoven. The programme
focuses on design practices attuned to ecological and social
challenges. In 2022, she received the Harvard Graduate
School of Design's Wheelwright Prize for a project on the future
of data storage. From 2015 to 2022, she was the director of
Research at Het Nieuwe Instituut where she led initiatives focused on labour, extraction and mental health from an architectural and post-anthropocentric perspective, including *Auto-
mated Landscapes* and *BURN-OUT.* Previously, she was
director of global network programming at Studio-X, Columbia
University Graduate School of Architecture, Planning and
Preservation, New York. Otero was co-curator of the Shanghai
Biennial 2021, curator of the Dutch Pavilion at the Venice
Architecture Biennale 2018, and chief curator of the 2016 Oslo
Architecture Triennale. She has co-edited the publications

Lithium: States of Exhaustion (2021), *A Matter of Data* (2021), *More-than-Human* (2020), *Architecture of Appropriation* (2019), *Work, Body, Leisure* (2018) and *After Belonging* (2016), among others. Her PhD thesis *Evanescent Institutions* (2016) examines the emergence of new paradigms for institutions and, in particular, the political implications of temporal and itinerant structures.

IMAGE CREDITS

1   Reinhold Rossig, Untitled (writing exercise, assignment by Joost Schmidt at the Bauhaus Dessau), 1929. Gouache on paper, 42,0 x 29,3 cm. Bauhaus Dessau Foundation, I 6184/13 G.

2   R. Buckminster Fuller and Shoji Sadao with June Jordan, Harlem Skyrise Project (detail), c. 1960. Courtesy Columbia University Graduate School of Architecture, Planning and Preservation.

3   Building of the apprentice schools in Bratislava (detail), 1930s. Black and white photograph, Archive of Iva Mojžišová - Slovak Design Centre

4   Close-up of a woman at work inside the Design Laboratory's shop facilities. (Courtesy of the United States National Archives and Records Administration).

5   Student work by Hans von Klier from the Maldonado Basic Course, 1955-1956. HfG Ulm Archive.

6   Hermelindo Flaminghi, *Noigandres* 4 magazine cover, 1954. (personal archive)

7   Detail from: Dorothy Jackson, 'The Black Experience in Graphic Design', in: *Print Magazine* XXII:VI 1968.

8   Carrie Mae Weems, Untitled (Woman brushing hair), 1990.

9   Detail from cover, Victor J. Papanek: *Design for Human Scale*, 1983. Courtesy, Papanek Foundation, University of Applied Arts Vienna.

10   Kunstgewerbemuseum Berlin, project documentation 'Neobionten. Design Lab #9', 2021.

11   Construction work in the former Termokos factory. Photographer: Enzo Leclerq.

12   *New World Embassy: Rojava*, a project by Democratic Self-Administration of Rojava & Studio Jonas Staal at the Oslo Architecture Triennale 2016 curated by After Belonging Agency (Lluís Casanovas, Ignacio Galán, Carlos Mínguez, Alejandra Navarrete and Marina Otero). Photograph by Istvan Virag.

SCHOOLS OF DEPARTURE

#1 Decolonising design education
#2 The New Designer: Design as a profession

All issues can be found under:
atlas.bauhaus-dessau.de/en/journal

The *Schools of Departure* series is published in connection with the homonymous online research platform, a digital atlas established by the Bauhaus Dessau Foundation with the objective to map experiments in art and design education beyond the Bauhaus. These experiments are understood as manifestations of travelling concepts which, with ever-shifting connotations, keep a wide variety of educational approaches in a process of constant exchange and motion. Studying these phenomena through the lens of travelling concepts such as Decolonisation, New Designers, New Communities, Creativity, Craft, Science, or Deschooling enables us to explore narratives around 'routes of appropriation' that move between different geographies, times and cultures.

This book aggregates a selection of texts that have initially been created for the online research platform in late 2022. It constitutes one of two inaugural issues of the series, with new volumes to appear on a yearly basis.

The online research platform *Schools of Departure* was partly funded in 2021 in the context of the Digital Agenda for the State of Saxony-Anhalt with funds from the Ministry of Infrastructure and Digital Affairs of the State of Saxony-Anhalt. In 2022, the project has been further developed as part of *dive in. Programme for Digital Interactions* of the Kulturstiftung des Bundes (German Federal Cultural Foundation) with funding by the Federal Government Commissioner for Culture and the Media (BKM) through the NEUSTART KULTUR programme.

atlas.bauhaus-dessau.de

Gropiusallee 38
06846 Dessau-Roßlau
Germany
represented by:
Director and CEO
Barbara Steiner

Regina Bittner, Katja Klaus,
Catherine Nichols, and Philipp Sack

Philipp Sack

Frederik Richthofen

Offshore, (Isabel Seiffert and
Christoph Miler), offshorestudio.ch

Leonardo Angelucci, 0x000.ch

Gutenberg Beuys Feindruckerei
GmbH, Langenhagen

Spector Books
Harkortstrasse 10, 04107 Leipzig
www.spectorbooks.com

Germany, Austria: GVA,
    Gemeinsam
    Verlagsauslieferung
    Göttingen GmbH&Co. KG,
    www.gva-verlage.de
Switzerland: AVA
    Verlagsauslieferung AG,
    www.ava.ch
France, Belgium: Interart Paris,
    www.interart.fr
UK: Central Books Ltd,
    www.centralbooks.com
USA, Canada, Central and South
America, Africa: ARTBOOK/ D.A.P.,
    www.artbook.com
South Korea: The Book Society,
    www.thebooksociety.org
Japan: twelvebooks,
    www.twelve-books.com
Australia, New Zealand:
    Perimeter Distribution,
    www.perimeterdistribution.com

First Edition, 2023
Printed in Germany
© Bauhaus Dessau Foundation
ISBN 978-3-95905-748-6

The Bauhaus Dessau Foundation is
a non-profit foundation under public
law. It is institutionally funded by:

Die Beauftragte der Bundesregierung
für Kultur und Medien

SACHSEN-ANHALT
#moderndenken

Dessau
⌐ Roßlau